Seasons *of a* Mother's Heart

Seasons *of a* Mother's Heart

❦

Heart~to~Heart Encouragement

for Homeschooling Moms

Sally Clarkson

Whole Heart Ministries

Keeping Faith in the Family

SEASONS OF A MOTHER'S HEART
Copyright © 1998, 2008 by Sally Clarkson
Published by Whole Heart Ministries
P.O. Box 3445, Monument, CO 80132
www.wholeheart.org

ISBN-13: 978-1-888692-17-4
ISBN-10: 1-888692-17-0

Unless otherwise indicated, all Scripture taken from the HOLY BIBLE, NEW INTERNATIONAL VERSION ®. NIV ®. Copyright 1973, 1978, 1984 by International Bible Society. Used by permission of Zondervan. All rights reserved. (www.Zondervan.com).

Scripture quotations marked NASB taken from the New American Standard Bible®, Copyright © 1960, 1962, 1963, 1968, 1971, 1972, 1973, 1975, 1977, 1995 by the Lockman Foundation. Used by permission. (www.Lockman.org)

Cover design by Mike Cox, Alpha Advertising, Sidell, Illinois

Whole Heart Press is a division of Whole Heart Ministries, a non-profit, 501(c)(3) Christian home and parenting ministry dedicated to encouraging and equipping Christian parents to raise wholehearted Christian children at home. For more information, visit the ministry website at www.wholeheart.org.

Printed in the United States of America
Second Edition
2008—First Printing

CONTENTS

Preface to New Edition.. vii

Introduction: Seasons of My Heart........................... 13

Spring: Season of Renewal.. 21

1. Celebrating Life.. 31

2. Changing My Will... 45

3. Beside Still Waters 59

Summer: Season of Response 75

4. Building Your House... 85

5. Planning to Live 99

6. Surprised by Joy 115

Fall: Season of Resolve 133

7. A Touch of Sympathy.. 143

8. Freedom from Guilt.. 159

9. Living with Discipleship 175

Winter: Season of Reflection 195

10. Prayers from Home.. 205

11. Light in the Darkness.. 219

12. Enduring with Grace.. 235

Postscript 251

This book is dedicated to my precious mother, Wanda,

whose encouraging words, gentle hands,

and generous heart have inspired me

to embrace with joy

the biblical calling

of motherhood.

1998

❤

2008

May God bless

my sweet daughters, Sarah

and Joy, and my future daughters

in-law, to be mothers who will faithfully

serve the Lord by serving their children, and may

they always know his joy through all the seasons of life.

Preface to New Edition

I am sitting in my bedroom today peering out on a misty, cool fall morning. A cup of coffee is in my hand as I sit here listening to soft instrumental music, enjoying the flicker of my candles, and pondering how far this road of motherhood has brought me in the last ten years. It has been a decade since I first wrote *Seasons of a Mother's Heart*. As I look back, I realize that I was just beginning to understand then the many seasons of life mothers go through—the ups and downs, the beauty and the battle, the alternating confidence and doubt through which I would travel. I was also beginning to sense a deep conviction that homeschooling mothers, especially, needed to be affirmed for their decision to home educate, and to feel validated for the unique pressures of the lifestyle they had taken on.

Of course, I have always applauded all mothers who give generously of their lives to their children, and have affirmed the importance of God's biblical design for motherhood in several other books I have written since this book was first released. And yet, after twenty years of living and learning at home, I feel even more strongly that homeschooling mothers, like me, need a specific kind of encouragement. There is not a lot in our contemporary culture to acknowledge or affirm the unique journey we have chosen in raising our children at home for God's glory.

It was in such a spirit that I began to write this book the first time back in 1997. I wanted to give encouragement and support especially to homeschooling moms, and to be a voice for them. However, I have been so personally encouraged to discover that moms from all walks of life, whether or not they homeschool, have found *Seasons* to be a source of support and encouragement for them, too. Moms with vastly differing educational points of view have told me over the years how very much this book has meant to them, and even some how they have practically memorized chapters from reading them so much. Both homeschooling and non-homeschooling moms have commented on the encouragement it has brought to them. I am so very grateful for the many letters and emails I have received from moms who wanted me to know how the book has impacted their lives.

Sacrificial motherhood is a universal drive, and I believe we are all closely connected by the reality of gracious mother-love for our children. It is part of God's design. In our own countries, times, and homes, whether American or not, homeschooler or not, we are all involved in a great work that was on the very heart of God from the beginning of creation.

❧

This book first took shape in a tiny, five-by-four foot enclosed garret above the staircase in my mother's condominium in Norman, Oklahoma, where she had moved after my father died. While my mom attempted to keep my four wiggle-worms contented and occupied, I would hide behind the closed door of my "writing closet" so I could frantically write down the thoughts that would eventually become a book. At that time my children were 13, 10, 8, and 2. Since those busy days I have lived through the roller-coaster years of teenage hormones, driver's licenses, and SATs, and ushered at least a couple of my children into young adulthood. Clay and I have also weathered four more moves, passed the quarter century mark in our marriage, and, much to our sadness, have no more elementary school-age children in our home. I realize now what a special time the season of innocent childhood is in the life of a mother.

My own sweet mother, at 85, has been declining in health for several years now, and doesn't even remember the sacrifices she made for me through so many years of my childhood, or even in the writing of this book. I am not even sure she always knows who I am when I call her on the phone. Yet the imprint of her hands, her voice, and her love are still here, stored in my heart, living through me as I love my own children. Whatever inadequacies or failure there were in my own family-life from childhood, they have now been covered with the grace of God's love and the gift of forgiveness which has been born in my heart through the reality of Jesus. I am left remembering the love and beauty I have been given. No mom alive will ever be perfect or always adequate, but for those who serve in a spirit of love and joy, there will always be strings of loving connection between the heart of a child and her mom, tying them together forever.

And so, as I have gone back to re-visit the pages of this book after ten years, I have realized that it is that same love and grace that endure through every stage of motherhood. The biblical principles I wrote about are still true and apply to my life today—choosing to be content, learning to reach for God instead of happiness, celebrating life with my children, learning to endure with grace. As I reflect on what has changed between the first writing of this book and the present, though, I have to say that the main change has been my perspective on life as a mother.

When I look at my own mother now, I can see clearly that my designated time in which to be productive is limited. There are, really, only a few years left for me to be an active mother. I see my own grown children and my quickly-growing last child, Joy, and I understand that life really does fly quickly by. It really is crucial that I make the most of every moment and learn to enjoy, inspire, and encourage every chance I get, because soon the minutes will all be gone. I know this all too well as my oldest children are caught up in life outside of my home, and they are beginning to enter into their work and the life that God is opening up before them.

With this perspective in mind, though, I find that I am more patient with the difficulties, probably because I am more familiar with them for having lived through them! I give more grace to my children, because I see that they really do grow up, even if I have not always invested as much as I would have liked to in them. They just move on, as God has prepared them to do, according to the established limit of time. I understand so much more deeply now that the things that really mean the most are love and deep relationships, the well-living of mundane life, the discussions around the dinner table, and the sharing of memories and celebrations that have knit our hearts together. The foundations of our family have always been our love for God and our love for each other, and I have watched as these values cemented us together as a family. I greatly relish the fact that all of our children still look to home as the best place to be, and continue to return here to live again and again. Through all the ups and downs of our lives I wasn't sure how it would turn out, but now, I am so deeply thankful for the connectedness and grace we share.

At this end of things, having traveled and known more people, and read more deeply, I have seen that "life" is not primarily about me or my own. I am just a part of a much greater history of a people who were created to choose how they would invest and use the few short years of their life on earth. That investment could be for God, for his kingdom, and for a legacy for eternity. Or, it could be for temporal things, and experiences that cannot be kept, and that will not fulfill. All beautiful, or rich, or famous people still eventually get old and sick, and die. Yet the choices that all people (and perhaps especially mothers!) have made in the midst of their seasons of life will determine whether their life's messages will have an eternal impact after they are gone, or fade with time and simply be forgotten.

To a great extent, the messages and values of parents will be lived out through those children who have grown in and accepted what their parents have lived and taught at home. But this will happen only if they have made the choice to live purposefully through the moments of time they have with their children in this journey of parenting. However great the messages of life, and however strong the values a parent holds, they will be rejected and lost by children whose hearts and lives were more imprinted by culture, than by their own home. If the personal time and love of a parent was not given in integrity, the values close to their heart will not be passed on or accepted by their children.

In this way, I see more and more that the family indeed matters in God's scheme of things. As the family goes, so goes the culture. That is why the homeschooling movement has been such a blessing to me and to our family. It was through the structure of homeschooling that I truly learned the value of family. It was in the midst of homeschooling my children and having them present at every moment of my day that I learned to enjoy and value deeply the home fires and the intimacy of my relationship with them. My children have naturally become my best friends and heartfelt companions. Investing in their lives and enjoying their friendship became a deeply satisfying joy that I never expected.

What took more out of me, also gave more back to me. Studying great books and thoughts along with them developed me into a learner for life. Having great discussions, snuggling up together under sleeping bags to study the stars and tell funny stories, learning to work together in the midst of hundreds and hundreds of people in our home and at our conferences created strong bonds between our hearts. Taking trips all over the U.S. and the world, and sharing in memories and experiences because we had time to be together, was far more fulfilling than I could ever have known when I first began. Talking about the truths of God's word, his purposes, and his love became the life values that we all shared because we did everything and valued everything together. Motherhood has become more of a deeply satisfying calling than I could ever have imagined.

I don't think I could possibly have experienced the depths of these joys and relationships if I hadn't had my children with me all the time, away from the competition of outside voices and time constraints. We were a little "club" of people who lived as all-for-one and one-for-all. My children have become mature companions who share my tastes in life, food, books, and experiences. We are best friends who have forged through the many difficulties of life and become a team strongly connected by our shared commitments. How wonderful God intended family to be, and what blessings and stability and comfort he provided in this design. But that divine design for home and family only really became clear to me as a result of homeschooling. It really is not about the education or the curriculum, but about the value and essence of life itself.

And so, with the memory of all that life around me, I dedicate this new "Ten Year Anniversary" edition of *Seasons of a Mother's Heart* to all of you moms who have made the choice to homeschool. You have gone against the grain of culture in order to take on the challenging but rewarding task of educating your children at home. You have chosen to give up your time, freedom, comfort, and "normal" adult life in order to live, learn, love, and labor with your children at home. I believe history will be different because of you—moral characters will be stronger, biblical family values preserved, and God's name honored. Future generations will follow the Lord and build on biblical foundations because of the choices and sacrifices you have made. Make no mistake, your investment will last for all of eternity. I am blessed to be part of such a wise, strong, and inspirational group of women. I applaud your choice and I commend you into the hands of our loving God, who is so willing to bless, and love, and strengthen you!

This new "Ten Year Anniversary" edition includes four new chapters, introducing the Spring, Summer, Fall, and Winter sections. These new essays are written from a "ten years later" personal perspective. The introduction, original twelve chapters, Bible studies, and the postscript are substantially as they were written "ten years before" (with some gentle editing). I hope you will gather some friends, read *Seasons* together, and do the Bible study and discussion questions. We have heard through the years about "*Seasons* groups" of homeschooling moms all around the country, so we're praying that God will spread the word and start a whole new round of groups for a new generation of homeschooling mothers. Please let me know if you start a group! Wholehearted blessings and grace to you on your exciting journey of Christian motherhood and homeschooling.

Sally Clarkson
November 25, 2007

Introduction ~ Seasons of My Heart

Finishing a book like this is like having a baby—it's in the womb for a long time, then there is a whole lot of work and pain for a short time, and finally you can hold your baby in your hands. I certainly feel that joy at getting this book birthed. It has taken a much longer time than I anticipated to get it out, but I am so excited to be able to hold it in my hands. I pray that God will use it to minister to you, and to many other homeschooling mothers.

That's one baby birthed, but I feel like I've got another one on the way right on this one's heels. You see, even as I write this introduction, we are in labor to give birth to our first WholeHearted Mother Conference, "Renew My Heart O Lord." We're down to the "short time," and it is a whole lot of work and pain, but I am so excited at what God is doing! About 650 homeschooling mothers are coming from over a dozen states for a Friday night and all day Saturday conference designed just for them. It will be a time of inspiration, motivation, and spiritual renewal.

I mention the conference only to illustrate that the Spirit of God is moving among homeschooling mothers. It has been on my heart since we started Whole Heart Ministries four years ago to minister to the spiritual needs of mothers who are giving their lives in service to their children. I know how much I need to be refreshed and encouraged in the Lord, and I think the response to our WholeHearted Mother Conference speaks loudly that other homeschooling mothers feel the same way.

This book, *Seasons of a Mother's Heart*, is my attempt to speak in print to the needs of those mothers. My goal is not to be a cheerleader for homeschooling, but to come alongside you as a fellow homeschooling mother and share the burden of motherhood. My desire is to talk about the heart issues of the homeschooling lifestyle. I have tried to share out of my own experiences about both the victories and defeats, the joys and struggles, and the successes and failures. These are the things that I would want to talk about if you and I could sit down over tea for a visit...things of the heart.

This book is a continuation of what was started in *The WholeHearted Mother Journal*, an eight-page quarterly newsletter that we published for a year until God showed me it was taking me away from my children (see chapter 2, Changing My Will). Four essays originally published in the *Journal* have been lengthened and included; the rest are new for the book. Though I could no longer write and publish a newsletter, I had so many homeschooling mothers write to tell me how much the essays had encouraged them, helped them put the stresses of their lives in perspective, and pointed them back to the real, biblical priorities of motherhood. I really loved the newsletter, but Clay encouraged me to take my time and write a book of essays.

Let me include an aside here to the many wonderful women who have taken the time to write to me in response to the newsletter, a workshop, or one of our books. I have so enjoyed getting your letters in my mailbox, and I would so love to answer personally each one I receive. However, I have found that I am not able to answer all the letters I receive and maintain my priorities at home. That is frustrating for me since I consider each woman who writes to be a friend in the Lord. If I have failed to answer your letter, just know that I answered it in my heart. And please keep writing!

ॐ

The more I study the Bible, the more I see the beautiful design of God for mothers. Our role, as God intended and designed it, is so important in the process of raising a godly child. And yet what should bring great blessing and joy often brings great burden, partly because homeschooling is hard work, but also because the traditional role of the mother is under attack in our culture.

By staying home to homeschool, you are going against the grain of social norms. That fact alone, even without the physically tiring realities of the homeschool lifestyle, will eventually wear on you emotionally and spiritually. Choosing to embrace what culture condemns, even though it is blessed by God, can be a heavy cross to bear.

The more I study the Bible, though, the more I also am reminded of what it is I really need as a homeschooling mother—the ministry of the Holy Spirit, the power of prayer, the provision of grace, and the life of faith. When I need encouragement to persevere, I need the light of God's truth shining on the shadowy places in my heart. I need the gentle admonition of the Holy Spirit to run the race with endurance. I need to be transformed by the renewing of my mind with God's purpose for mothers, fathers, and children.

What I have tried to do in this book is acknowledge the burdens and difficulties of being a homeschooling mother, but even more to point you to the biblical answers for how to do God's will for your life with confidence and joy. That, to me, is the real challenge of the homeschooling lifestyle— to maintain a living and vibrant faith in the power of the Holy Spirit.

It may not need to be said, but this book is not a comprehensive "study" of how to do that. It is just a collection of essays written from my heart that talk about a wide variety of spiritual topics. I have no systematic agenda to promote, no doctrinal axe to grind, and no sacred cows to attack. I just had some things I wanted to say to other homeschooling mothers like myself. I have no desire to lay more burden on you, or give you more things to do. I simply want to offer some help and hope in the midst of this difficult, but fulfilling, life we have chosen.

Introduction

When I first thought about this book, I envisioned it being not just a book to read, but a book to be used as well. I saw it used with a Bible in hand encouraging a homeschooling mother in her quiet time. I saw it used as a discussion guide for a monthly fellowship of homeschooling moms. I saw it used as a source of new, practical ideas for how to grow as a mother.

Whether every chapter hits the mark in your heart, or just some, or even just one, my greatest desire is that God will make this book useful in your life. I hope you will let me know if and how God uses something in this book in your life.

৵

My prayer is that this book, in some small way, will encourage and perhaps even enable you to find a new freedom and spiritual strength in your role as a mother. I pray that you will discover a renewed sense of fulfillment and joy as a mother, but even more I pray that your children will be the real beneficiaries as you raise them up to become godly leaders for the next generation.

May God touch your heart with his truth as you read, and may the children you raise up for the Lord "rise up and call you blessed."

Sally Clarkson
January 16, 1998

Seasons *of a* Mother's Heart

Spring ~ Season *of* Renewal

Spring
Reflections on Renewal
Ten Years Later

May twenty-sixth dawned a beautiful spring day. The wildflowers we had planted as seeds in February were already sprouting in some places, the young aspen trees were blowing gently in the soft wind, and the purple columbines were in full bloom. It was a blue and pearl sky day that rained a gentle light down on the mountain meadow next to our home with its myriad of tiny white flowers swaying as though dancing in the breeze. The iridescent mountain blue jays were squawking in the trees as though ready to celebrate the warm days of late spring so longingly expected.

As I sipped my coffee out on the deck of our mountain home, I was filled with thanksgiving for the sheer glory of the day. My four sweet ones were reveling in the joy of the morning below me, whooshing through the air on their swings, clambering up the tree house, and testing their strength on the monkey bars.

"We'd better get going on our day," I yelled down from my observation station on the deck above them. "Come and join me!" Seeking to ease into the day with our morning devotion, I opened my Bible to the Psalms and felt as though the one I found had been written and planned just for us:

"The heavens are declaring the glory of God…"

Sarah, Joel, Nathan, and Joy were also declaring their delight and pleasure in God's gift of this warm day after a winter and spring of heavy snow. Everything about the morning seemed to reflect the touch of God's creative fingers. Breathless with her excitement, Joy bounced up to me, leaned on my knees with wide eyes full of delight.

"Wow, Mommy," she squeaked in her sweet, four-year-old voice. "I think the mountain is declarin' the glory, too! Do you think Jesus made this a 'specially pretty day 'cause it's my birthday?"

"Well, maybe he did!" I declared with the very last sip of my coffee, rewarded by Joy's sweet grin.

A glance at my watch broke the mood. I was almost reluctant to leave the peace of the moment for what lay ahead, but I had invited three other little girls and one little boy to come to a small birthday party to celebrate the afternoon with Joy. I realized that I needed to kick into my Martha gear if I was ever going to get everything ready for the party. It seemed such a shame to leave the refreshment of such a beautiful morning in order to attack the work that was ahead of me, but I wanted this day to be special for Joy. I assured myself that it would all be worth the effort.

The moms of Joy's little friends would probably stay during the party and I had a lot of work to do before they came. My list of expectations seemed to grow longer the longer I sat. I hadn't noticed those dead leaves under the doorstep before now. As I walked into the kitchen, I noticed that there were black and smeary fingerprints along the edge of the pantry where my less than sterile children had opened the door with food-covered hands. The cake needed to be frosted and decorated, the rooms straightened up and vacuumed, and the breakfast dishes in the sink dealt with. And, the hidden presents in my closet were still unwrapped. I entered the restroom only to find that there was no paper in the holder, clothing had been thrown in the corner from the shower the night before, and the sink still showed the remains of toothpaste never washed away. I sighed. I simply wouldn't look anymore. I might see one more thing to do. As I exited the bathroom, I gathered my young house servants to me. My adrenalin was already beginning to race.

"Listen to me!" I barked, as though somehow my authoritative voice would extract greater maturity from my immature house cleaners than normal. "We have an awful lot of work to do today to make sure that this house is clean, and to get ready for Joy's birthday party, and I expect each of you to be a big help."

I began to parcel out the jobs. Sarah was assigned to decorating the dining room where the festivities would take place. Joel got taping balloons and curly ribbons onto the back of Joy's birthday chair. I would oversee the setting out of the special Winnie the Pooh plates, napkins, and cups along with small bowls of candy and finger food. Joy's current ideal menu included little triangle sandwiches, strawberries and grapes, "goldfish" snack crackers, and chocolate cake. Then I appended to each of those tasks the list of responsibilities from my previous walk through the house.

"Let's get going!" I said, in my best motivational voice.

Because Joy kept tagging along behind me as I worked, asking me to play with her since "this is my special day," I searched my mind to figure out what she could do to keep her occupied away from me. I was doing all of this for her, after all, I told myself. I finally retrieved one of the party favors from the shopping bag and presented it to her with great ceremony, hoping it would keep her occupied outside so that I could get all the work done. Starting when Sarah was little, I had discovered that one of the best favors for little kid birthday parties was a plastic pinwheel on a stick that would spin in the air with a gentle blow. I had found a deal on them at a local store and had picked them up for Joy's birthday, hoping she would find them as delightful as the other kids had at her age. I led her out on the deck and showed her how the little fan-on-a-stick would spin in the wind. She was wildly delighted and immediately captivated.

For the next hour I rushed through all the work, managing to make my three older kids miserable as I heaped them all with guilt over the need to work harder and to "never, never, *never* close the kitchen door with dirty fingers ever again!" Finally we reached the ten-minute mark until the party began, and I hurried everyone to their bedroom to don their party clothes.

"Where's Joy?" I asked, glancing through the house.

"She's out in the front yard, still running with the pinwheel."

I raced upstairs onto the deck, swept her up in my arms, and hurried her upstairs to her bedroom to get her out of her comfy clothes into her party gear. "Oh, Mommy," she sighed, "do I have to come in? I was having so much fun!"

The party began, and the next hours were a mad dance of stress and disappointment. One little girl cried without ceasing all afternoon, first because she wasn't sitting next to Joy, next because she didn't like the piece of cake I gave her, and finally because another child fought back when she pushed him off his chair. The lone boy attending the bash grew tired of the girl's timidity and decided to liven things up by exuberantly flinging a toy truck through the air. It struck one of the cups with a satisfying crash and sent red juice spewing onto the carpet. The little girl whose juice it was set to howling because she wanted her own red juice back, not the silly orange juice which had replaced the grape. The gift opening was decidedly underwhelming, distracted as everyone was by the outbreak of a fight between two beribboned little girls to be the one to hold a little doll. In the midst of all this excitement, Joy kept sidling up to me, asking when the party would be over so that she could go back to having fun again.

Finally the last family left and I began to survey the damage. Now there was even more work to do, but (I thought with grim satisfaction) at least we had made the effort. I straightened up for a few minutes and then began to search for Joy to see if she had salvaged any fun from the wayward party. I stood for a moment listening for her voice, and was caught by the sound of something pattering repeatedly up and down our long deck. I recognized the sound of little feet echoing off the wooden rafters of our deck. I slipped outside, unnoticed by Joy, and sunk into a corner chair by my bedroom door.

There she was, my littlest birthday girl, arrayed in the faded and worn pink of her absolutely beloved ballet suit. With breathless excitement she was running the length of the 40-foot deck as fast as she could. She giggled with every single step, thrilled that her hearty motion set the sparkling little pinwheel to whirling in the warm air. She barely saw me, only aware of her own glee as she ran back and forth, forth and back, panting, watching, laughing.

I watched her for a full ten minutes, my weary feet propped on a footstool on the deck. Finally out of breath, Joy ran over and plopped into my lap. "Mommy, I am so glad everyone finally left so now I can really do what I want. Thank you so much for this pinwheel. It is the best present you ever got me! I love you! I'm so glad that finally just you and me can be together. It's still a glory day like you said this morning, right? This is my best part of the day!"

She jumped off my lap and continued pattering up and down with her pinwheel until the sun set behind the mountain and she could barely see the bright colors of the wheel anymore. Before it grew dark, though, I snuck into a corner with the video camera to record this memory that was already etched so permanently in my mind.

Here was this entirely un-self-conscious little girl, reveling in utter abandon in the delight of a simple moment outside. With her little treasure clutched in her hands and the wind blowing her light hair, she was perfectly happy. The wonder of the pleasure of her moments, and the beauty of the fresh spring day, filled her sweet eyes with innocent sparkles. I had spent almost the entire day in unnecessary preparations and guilt-producing chores, upsetting my entire household so that we could have the party just right. Yet I had neglected to take pleasure in the joy of a little girl who would not always be four years old, and who was completely delighted, quite apart from any effort of mine, to simply be alive in the beauty of a fresh spring day.

❀

The springtime of life in nature is when color and music invade the silent cold of winter. Flowers bloom in a profusion of beauty, green springs up everywhere, and birds trill songs to blue skies. The buds on trees burst out in color, proclaiming that everything isn't really dead, it just seemed that way for awhile, but now is the time for life. Spring has always been a time symbolic of birth—of babies being born and life beginning again, an endless circle of renewal assuring each new generation that life will continue in the years to come.

As I look back on the spring seasons of my life, especially the babyhood years, I wish that I had been more able to rejoice in them. I wish I had taken more time to see the pleasure of little children running in old ballet suits, delighting in the simple beauties of life, like the springtime wind, flowers blooming, lady bugs crawling, and pinwheels spinning. How I miss the quiet, miraculous times when my babies would happily pat my chest as they nursed contentedly at my breasts. How much pleasure I used to derive out of Sarah as a baby just rolling over for the first time, pushing her bottom into the air as she attempted to crawl, and the joy of her first step taken on her birthday combined with her first words of "Mama" (me!) and "Buppy" (the dog next door).

Looking back, I can see how I jumped into too many "busy" activities because I thought it was something we "should" do, or because my friends were doing it. In the end, many of those activities only added stress to my life and over-stimulated my children. I see so many young mothers now already worrying about their young children being behind in skills or academics at the age of five, and even younger. The pressure to conform, to be sure your child doesn't "miss out on anything," and to be sure they are not "falling behind," is constant and debilitating.

But there are so many amazing discoveries a child will make simply by being at home with his or her parents—exploring his world, pretending, playing with modeling clay, swinging on a swing, tinkering with simple toys, playing instruments and singing, listening for hours to books while cuddled in mom's lap. These are things that God built in the rhythm of normal life in a family, and they will build a rich soul. However, choosing to walk confidently in God's design requires a step of faith—a step away from the "marketplace" of activities, and into the "mommy-place" of the home, filled with beauty, love, creativity, purpose, and peace.

God has designed beauty and pleasure to inhabit the simplest of things, but we have to be still in our hearts to enjoy them. We have to submit and assent by faith to the reality of each day, however mundane, choosing to see with heart-eyes the reasons for thanksgiving and joy. Otherwise we miss the power of the spring seasons. Every new season or segment of life—newly weds, pregnancy, babies, toddlers, elementary school, hormones and teen years, graduating and leaving home, marriage all over again—are all spring seasons, springboards to new opportunities and adventures. Each of these times of life is pregnant with hope and life within them, and yet each of these spring seasons will also require some adjustments to change.

Spring is a picture of rebirth and resurrection. It proclaims anew each year that there is a powerful river of life ever flowing in God's nature, that can never be held back or stopped. Trees bloom, grass grows, flowers sprout, and birds come back to sing because God has made a beautiful rhythm of returning life. It is his design.

Spring is an invitation to enter into the joy of the psalmist with his proclamation: "This is the day the Lord has made; let us rejoice and be glad in it." (Psalm 118:24). It is the spirit of the new season and returning life.

In Luke 5:33-35, the Pharisees accuse the disciples of being far too joyful, and celebrating life too much, because they ate and drank with Jesus. These disciples had neglected to follow the legalistic ways of the Pharisees who judged people by their works, not by the attitude of their hearts. In the Pharisees' eyes, the disciples were failing in righteousness because they didn't work hard enough, or treat life as seriously as they ought to. Jesus' answer to them was, "You cannot make the attendants of the bridegroom fast while the bridegroom is with them, can you? But the days will come; and when the bridegroom is taken away from them, then they will fast in those days." In other words, "this is the day" to live and celebrate.

Our learning to celebrate life when God has given good things to us is a pleasure to him. We bring him joy by accepting the gladness found in the gifts he has provided. We will all walk through many seasons of springtime in our lives. They are the bright, innocent, promising days that can fill us up for the future if only we will enter into their joy and their adjustments with grace. Winter seasons will come into our lives. How important it is that we choose to celebrate beauty when we can, storing up joy and happiness to revisit in the cold of the winter nights ahead.

But even rejoicing requires a choice—we have to submit to the limitations of the spring years and seasons, we have to accept the small graces, and submit to the beautiful blooms and the little storms. We have to see spring as a gift of life, not a season to be endured, or even just passively experience. God invites us to look and to see with the eyes of our hearts all that is good, to find peace and rest as we see what is important, and to discard any things that would distract us from the life he offers. Spring is a time of living fully in the present, loving deeply, and celebrating the newness of life as it comes our way.

Spring

*Therefore, I urge you, brothers, in view of
God's mercy, to offer your bodies as living
sacrifices, holy and pleasing to God—this is
your spiritual act of worship.*

*Do not conform any longer to the pattern of
this world, but be transformed by the
renewing of your mind. Then you will be able
to test and approve what God's will is—his
good, pleasing and perfect will.*

Romans 12:1-2

"There is no human love like a mother's love. There is no human tenderness like a mother's tenderness...In all ages everywhere, the true children of a true mother 'rise up and call her blessed'; for they realize, sooner or later, that God gives no richer blessing to man than is found in a mother's love."

Henry Clay Trumbull
Hints On Child Training

Chapter One

Celebrating Life

Be joyful always; pray continually; give thanks
in all circumstances, for this is God's will for
you in Christ Jesus.

Monday morning was here again...*already*. I'd barely made a dent in my To Do list from last week, and now I had a whole new mental list that was growing longer with each room I walked through. Wherever I looked there was a project—put the library in order, organize the kitchen better, get the carpet cleaned, pick out toys to give away, thin out our clothes closets, put up new curtains, put all my paper piles into files, and on it went. What made my frustration meter climb steadily and head toward an inevitable overload, though, was the extra layer of mess that covered everything in every room.

Someone had detonated a stuff-bomb in our home over the weekend. It must have been a big one because the explosion had scattered its shrapnel to every corner of the house. Wherever I looked there were Lego pieces, little cars, piles of books and papers, mail stacks, newspapers, baby diapers, toys, orphan socks and shoes, unpacked backpacks, coffee cups, half-filled glasses, and at least a closet-full of discarded-where-it-was-removed clothing. My children seemed totally unaware of the messes around them as they played on the floor or read on the couch.

Of course, the house hadn't fallen apart in one weekend. We were still trying to recover from a year of expanding ministry, pregnancy, and birth after having added onto the existing family home when we moved to Walnut Springs, in central Texas. My frustration with never having my home "domain" in order had been building slowly over the previous months, but I had always been able to maintain some semblance of order, and so had been able to keep my frustration in check. Recently, though, after the birth of Joy, things had fallen more and more into disarray as I had turned my attention to the baby. As I surveyed the mess, and my mess-resistant children, it just pushed me over the edge.

My unsuspecting children didn't see it coming and had nowhere to hide as their gentle Mommy was transformed before them into Sergeant Mother. Barking out orders like a seasoned Drill Instructor, I sternly warned them, "I'm going next door and when I return I expect to see this mess cleaned up! This is unacceptable! Do you understand?" With fearful eyes and cowered postures, they soberly nodded and "yes mam'd" their acknowledgement of my orders. I turned and left with my armload of laundry, trailing a black cloud of gloom and doom (and clothes) behind me, still simmering in my parental indignation. I felt sure I would see some results. I was wrong.

When I returned, it was obvious that nothing had been accomplished in my absence. And worse, all my children had apparently deserted their jobs! They were nowhere to be seen or heard as I stood amidst the mess and felt my anger beginning to rise. I was still standing there in stunned silence when I heard peels of hysterical laughter coming from the bedroom. That did it…my frustration meter blew. As I marched with building fury toward the sounds, I reviewed my options for the strict discipline I would meet out to my insubordinate children.

As I stormed into the room, I saw three giggling children hovering over my bed. I had a full head of steam built up and a strong lecture on responsibility ready to go as soon as I had sufficiently chastised them for their disobedience. I was just about to unleash my fury when eight year-old Joel defused my wrath. Totally oblivious to my frustration, he blurted out through his big, easy smile, "Come quick, Mom! Joy has found her foot and she's trying to stick it in her mouth to eat it!"

As he turned to join the rest of my giggling troops, I looked over to the bed and saw what all the commotion was about. My three precious children had been captivated by an enchanting, happy little baby who had just discovered her foot. My heart instinctively knew that this was not a time for judgment, but rather for joy. It was a moment to celebrate and enjoy. I quickly made the adjustment—Sergeant Mother made a hasty retreat and gentle Mommy was back. Then, joining in with my mirthful mess-makers, we laughed out loud together on the bed at the amazing talent of our new family member, providentially named Joy.

&

A few years ago, harshness would have won out over happiness. I probably would have lost my temper, raised my voice and made everyone generally miserable. Several years ago at Christmas, I had planned a special time to bake cookies with the kids. I expected it to be a precious Christmas memory. I also expected to get twelve dozen cookies made for Christmas plates. I had melted some chocolate for making candy-coated pretzels and turned away to work on a batch of cookies in the oven. When I turned back around to see how the kids were doing, I reeled at what I saw. Nathan, three years old at the time, had used the melted chocolate as finger paints. It covered his hands, face, hair and clothes, not to mention the cabinets and floor. Unfortunately, my anger made a bigger mess out of the situation. I missed the joy of that moment, but time and experience have tempered my temper since then. Today, I would get a big laugh out of my chocolate-covered child and take a few snapshots. I would choose joy.

I am more convinced than ever that even in the midst of the mundane, burdensome, and oftentimes frustrating tasks of life allotted to me as a mother, God wants me to find his joy. He wants every single day of my life to be a celebration of his blessings, whether they are large or small. He wants me to celebrate life...the life he has given to me.

But what does it mean to "celebrate life"? Does it mean that I can let my house be a wreck so I can enjoy my children, or that I never have negative thoughts and attitudes, or that I never discipline my children? Does it mean that I simply overlook the myriad difficulties that inevitably spoil the best days, or that I ignore the burdens I carry as a stay-at-home mom, or that I close my eyes to intractable sins that won't go away?

Of course not! The joy-filled life is not found by trying to diminish my God-given responsibilities as a woman, wife, and mother, nor can I find joy merely by refusing to face the hard realities of life in a fallen world. There is a tension that God is asking me to acknowledge and accept—the tension between ideals and realities. True joy is found by living somewhere between the "ideal life" and "daily realities." That is where Jesus meets me, where his Holy Spirit empowers, and where I learn how to live the Christian life with supernatural joy.

To me, to "celebrate life" is simply a choice. Every day, God extends his hand to offer me the gift of another day to live. I have the choice to take that gift and turn it into 24 hours of real life in Christ, or just let it become another 24 hours lived in a broken world. If I choose to accept it—to tranform those minutes and hours into life lived for and with my Savior—I have the opportunity to see God at work, enjoy his presence, wonder at his creation, appreciate the expressions of his beauty and love, and touch the minds and hearts of my children with his reality. That's certainly what I desire, but it is a choice I have to make.

"But Sally," you may be thinking, "I'm a homeschooling mom. Between the responsibilities, burdens, difficulties and demands on my time, just when is it that I am supposed to celebrate life? It's a victory just to make it through the day!" Believe me, I share your feelings, but I also am confident in saying that *the homeschooling lifestyle is your best opportunity for celebrating life as God meant it to be.* If you make the choice, it can become a journey of joy!

I certainly have not become perfect in celebrating life every day, but I am getting better at it every day. Let me share with you two simple, biblical principles that are helping me to make the daily choice to live a joyful life.

Choose to be thankful

There is no Scripture I know of where God says it is okay to grumble, pout, or complain. I sure would like to find one, but it's not there (I'm still looking!). There are, however, plenty of verses where God says to be thankful. It's hard to miss Paul's meaning when he tells believers in the Thessalonian church to "Be joyful always; pray continually; give thanks in all circumstances, for this is God's will for you in Christ Jesus" (1 Thes. 5:16-18). In case you missed it, it is God's will for you to be thankful.

When I'm facing difficult circumstances, that can be a very annoying verse. "You mean," I cry out to God, "I should be thankful for my daughter's asthma?...for my washing machine that overflowed fifteen times last year on my new linoleum?...for our financial struggles?...for that difficult relationship that never goes away?" And God replies in my spirit, "Yes, that is exactly what I mean. Because when you are thankful, I can see that you are acknowledging my sovereign control over *all* the circumstances of your life, whether good or bad." Yes, that can be a very annoying verse.

If I consider the alternatives to being thankful, I can readily see God's point. When I pout instead of be joyful, grumble instead of pray, and complain instead of give thanks, I am in effect telling God that he is mishandling my life and I don't like it. At that point, I have ceased to put my faith in my sovereign Lord, and have chosen to put my faith in my circumstances. In other words, I am telling God, and myself, that if my circumstances change, then and only then can I be happy. Until then, I have nothing to be thankful for. And that, according to Paul, is when I step out of God's will.

My sinful heart might try to counter that it is the lousy circumstances that have caused me to be out of God's will, but that's just rationalization—it is my *response* to them that put me out of God's will. That is why God admonishes me to be joyful and to give thanks "in all circumstances." When I do that, no matter how bad the circumstances, I am acknowledging that he is in control. It is an act of faith. I can choose, by faith, to see God's hand within any and all of the circumstances of my life.

Job's testimony comes to mind here. When tested to the limits with the loss of everything he owned or held dear, his wife tested him even further by cajoling him to blame God for his miseries. Job, however, replied, "Shall we indeed accept good from God and not accept adversity?" He was right in the middle of God's will, not blaming his circumstances or cursing God, but rather placing his faith in his trustworthy Maker.

I am by nature strong-willed and idealistic, and for many years I was in the habit of telling God how I thought he should run my life. I was so willing to live by faith and to do whatever it took to do his will, yet God didn't seem willing to reciprocate by changing the negative circumstances and relationships in my life! There was a period of 12 years in our marriage when Clay and I experienced difficult circumstances almost as a way of life. Even though it was also a time of wonderful ministry experiences and much fruitful work, I seemed to find myself too often complaining to God about the difficulties, pleading with him to change our circumstances.

Now, as I look back over those years, I can see that I wasted a lot of time wanting God to change the very circumstances he wanted to use to prepare me for the ministry we're now enjoying. How thankful I am that I did not get my own way, but how I wish even more that I had not wasted so much precious time trying to! Much joy was missed during those years by not choosing to be thankful.

Life is not that much different now than it was then, but I am different now. We still have great blessings mixed with great difficulties, but I am learning, like Job, how to choose to be thankful for both. Rather than resisting the life God has given to me, I can choose to relax and release the stress of a busy life through a spirit of thankfulness, because I know that God is in control. And in that choice, I am discovering the joy that God has always wanted me to have. And for that I can joyfully say, "Thank you, Lord!"

Learn to be content

Contentedness has never been one of the top ten character qualities of American life. In fact, we (and our children) are constantly deluged with the message that it is good to want more than you have, and that more things, experiences, or abilities will make you happier and more fulfilled. Though it is never said quite so bluntly, our American way of life depends in large measure on those who will willingly and regularly break the tenth commandment by coveting their neighbor's possessions. It's no wonder that we're a bit uncomfortable when we start talking about being content with what we have.

It makes me uncomfortable when I face the truth that happiness is not found in getting what I want, but rather in giving up my expectations of getting what I want. I don't like facing the truth that living in a fallen world means that life will never be as perfect as I want it to be! But that is a part of living between the ideals and realities. I have come to realize, after much struggle, that I will spend the better part of my life adjusting my expectations to life's limitations, rather than having my expectations fulfilled. Yet that is the first step on the road to finding true contentedness—learning to accept those limitations as a normal part of this life.

Paul said, "I have learned to be content whatever the circumstances" (Philippians 4:11-13). His quiet, honest testimony is a forceful reminder to me that contentedness is never a gift or a given, but rather a learned condition. It is a fruit of the Spirit's work in my life as I live each day by faith, walking in his power. It isn't some kind of supernatural salve that I can ask God to apply to my heart, but a *learned* condition of depending upon God. As Paul goes on to say, "I can do everything through him who gives me strength." And if I learn to be content, by faith, joy will naturally follow. Like thankfulness, though, I have to *choose* to be content before I can know the joy.

As I have shared and counseled with other homeschooling mothers, contentedness seems to be an illusive ideal. For many it seems there is always something out there, just beyond their grasp, that they cannot have but that they believe will make them more happy and fulfilled if they could somehow get their hands on it. But they can't, and it leaves them feeling anxious, empty, and depleted. They reach, but they cannot grasp, not just for material things, but for expectations of how their lives could or should be.

As I have sought the input of seasoned homeschooling mothers on this issue, their response has been consistent. The only way to make it in this homeschooling life is to reach for God instead of reaching for happiness. Trying harder to be happy or content will not make you happy and content; trying harder to rest in God and depend upon his grace will. It is a spiritual issue, not a practical one. Contentedness will not come from being more organized, sleeping longer, being a better wife, having a better home, using better materials, having more time to yourself, or whatever it is you think might help. Contentedness is learned in the process of daily accepting life as God gives it to you, and adjusting your expectations to life's limitations.

If it is God's will for me to homeschool, then he is not asking me to do more than I am able (1 Corinthians 10:13), and he is not withholding from me anything that I truly need (Philippians 4:19; James 2:2-8). If I choose to, I can learn to be content with the life that God has given to me, whether I have a little or a lot to live it with. What keeps me from being content is not what God is or isn't supplying. The real problem is that I, Sally, will not adjust my expectations to life's limitations—I want more than I can have, ask for more than I need, strive for more than I can do, and expect more than God has promised.

Once, I thought I had to have it all together—life, home, schooling, marriage, family—to be a good homeschooling mother. In fact, I thought I would be happier if I did. Now I know better. I know the limitations. I know that my house will be messier if it is populated round-the-clock by children. I know no matter how tight the schedule my schooling times will still be interrupted. I know that my less-than-perfect children will not always respond to my less-than-perfect discipline and instruction. I know that we will do well in some areas, and that we won't do well in others. I know that I will not always be the perfect wife and Clay will not always be the perfect husband. I know that we cannot afford the kind of house, or car, or vacations, or luxuries, or even some simple pleasures that I would like. But in all of that, I know that it's okay.

These are limitations I must live with. The more I resist them, the less contented I will be. But the more I learn to accept those limitations, and live within them, the more contented I will become. It's that simple.

❧

It all comes down to this—joy is the result of the choices that you make. If you are choosing to be thankful and learning to be content, then you are opening your heart to that joy. It is not a supernatural feeling that God pours on you from heaven, but a gift of the Holy Spirit that is released by faith (Galatians 5:22). You don't have to wait for God to give you joy, because it is already within you. You simply need to get your self out of the way and let the Spirit fill your heart and mind with his truth. That is exactly what you are doing when you choose to thank God and be content in all circumstances. You are exercising faith, and that faith releases the joy of the Spirit into your life. Only through the Holy Spirit can you truly celebrate life and find the joy God wants you to know.

Granted, that is not always *easy* with so many worries and responsibilities that get in the way of joy, but it is always *possible*. I will always have a picture in my mind of me and my children, close together on the bed, giggling at a little 18-pound bundle of Joy eating her foot. But that memorable moment of celebration started with a choice—that memories with my children are more important than their messes.

I have no assurance that I'll have another sweet baby to enjoy. My children will never again be just the way they are now. I don't know if we'll all be here together next Christmas, or even next week. But I do know that we are a family now, today, this moment, and I can celebrate each minute as it unfolds. It's my choice.

My joy isn't dependent upon getting my house as orderly as I would like, or upon getting the things we don't yet have that I can put in it, or upon getting all the schooling done, or anything else on my To Do list. My joy is dependent upon my relationship with my Lord, and our celebration together of this life he has given to me.

So make the choice to celebrate life with your family. It is so easy to think that life consists of the assorted responsibilities, tasks, and crises that fill up the hours of each homeschooling day. But it doesn't. The part of life that matters most are the moments and memories that happen each day...the ones that won't be forgotten.

So choose to be thankful, and learn to be content. You'll find the journey of joy that God wants you to know.

❧

Thoughts On the Living Word

God never assures us that the Christian life will be easy. Quite the opposite, it seems he goes out of his way to let us know it will be difficult. On the other hand, the Scriptures are filled with promises and expressions of the joy that is ours as believers. That seeming paradox is nowhere better expressed than in our Lord, "who for the joy set before him endured the cross." Christianity does not give me an easier life, but it does give me a better way to live. It does not make me a happier person, but it gives me a reason to be joyful. The joy of the Lord—born of the hope of eternal glory—should be the mark of every true believer.

Ecclesiastes 3:9-15

The writer of Ecclesiastes puts all of life into perspective in this passage. If the things of this world are "beautiful" yet we have "eternity" written on our hearts, how will that affect our view of life? Why has God given us good things to enjoy if they are only temporal? What will "endure forever" from the life God wants us to enjoy? What will endure forever from your family?

Philippians 4:10-13

Paul, thankful for the Philippians' gift, explains that he is content whatever his situation. What circumstances is God using in your life to help you "learn" to be content? How do you know that you would you be content whether you were "in need" or if you had "plenty"? How are you modeling to your children that you "can do everything through him who gives me strength"?

1 Thessalonians 5:16-18

What most often keeps you from experiencing joy? What would you need to do to be one who prays "continually"? What are the areas in your own life for which God wants you to give thanks, even though they are difficult? Do you believe you can do "God's will" according to this verse? Why, or why not?

Nehemiah 8:1-12

When Ezra the priest read God's word, the "Book of the Law," to the Jews who had returned to Jerusalem from Babylon, the people wept with sadness. How did Nehemiah, the governor, encourage them? If you were grieving, how would his words encourage you? How can rejoicing in God give you strength in the midst of life's difficulties?

My Thoughts

Thoughts On Living the Word

When I am starting to feel down or depressed, I need to have the Word of God where I can see it, like on a 3x5 card on the refrigerator. Sometimes, a quick reading of a verse such as 1 Thessalonians 5:16-18 is all I need to get back on track spiritually. I find that particular verse is also an easy one to memorize and keep at the front of my mind. ❧ Occasionally I will have a quiet time during which I write down all that I am thankful for, and especially for the things I appreciate about Clay and the children. It helps me focus on the positive things in my life. Or, I may write down whatever is keeping me from having the joy of the Lord in my life, and then I look for specific ways I can make changes in my life. ❧ As a pro-active way to keep the joy in my life, I'll plan at least one family activity each week that I know will be enjoyable for everyone. It's kind of a celebration of being a family—a walk in the park, family tea time or hot chocolate by the fire, a bike ride on the nature trail, or a special story time.

My Life

Personal application: Make a time to record in your spiritual journal all the things for which you are most thankful, not only for what you have, but also for what you don't have. Use the list each day this week in a quiet time to thank God for your blessings.

Family application: Plan a fun family event this week. Declare it to be a special time of celebration for something out of the norm—Third Child Awareness Week, Pet Night, Ice Cream Appreciation Day. It can be serious or silly, but build it up all through the week.

"We grow spiritually by obeying God through the words of Jesus being made spirit and life to us, and by paying attention to where we are, not to whether we are growing or not. We grow spiritually as our Lord grew physically, by a life of simple, unobtrusive obedience."

Oswald Chamber
My Utmost for His Highest

Chapter Two

Changing My Will

*For I have come down from heaven not to do
my will but to do the will of him who sent me.*

As I snuggled down in my comfortable teatime chair, an afternoon cup of English Breakfast tea in one hand and a Bible in the other, I closed my eyes and breathed out some of the tension I felt inside. God often meets me there in my times of quiet reflection and prayer, ministering to my needs or preparing my heart for something new. I hoped before I got back up again from my chair this time that I would also have in my hands some much-needed wisdom from the Lord.

The past two years had been a whirlwind of changes, challenges, and children. After twenty years of serving God through other people's ministries, Clay and I had stepped off the ledge of faith to start our own ministry. The stepping off wasn't so hard, but it had felt like one long freefall since.

It all started simply enough with our WholeHearted Child Workshops. Soon, the workshop notes expanded into a book, *Educating the Whole-Hearted Child*, and we became a publisher. The book generated our first Whole Heart Catalog. Also in that first year after the birth of our ministry, I gave birth to a new baby, Joy, after three miscarriages and well into my forties. Then came speaking opportunities, the WholeHearted Mother Workshop in our church (before the conferences), a second catalog, and an extensive rewrite of the book. And in the midst of all that, we launched a newsletter, the *WholeHearted Mother Journal*.

The idea of a newsletter to homeschooling mothers had been percolating in our minds from the beginning. At the time, it seemed like such a natural response to the steady stream of letters we were receiving from mothers who had responded to our ministry. Though his plate was already full with the catalog and the book rewrite, Clay agreed to design and edit the journal if I would do the writing and information gathering. We naively thought a quarterly newsletter would not require that much work.

It didn't take long for the stream of letters to become a river as I began to hear from like-minded moms responding to my newsletter. It was very gratifying to discover I was ministering to others, but it was just as encouraging to find a "fellowship in print" with women from all across America and even overseas who were journeying on the same pilgrimage of homeschooling with me. I took great delight in the growing number of subscriptions, closing in on 1,000 in just a few months, knowing that my new circle of fellowship was widening every day.

Growth of a ministry, though, as we soon learned, can be both a blessing and a burden. The realities of publishing a periodical began to weigh heavily on our lives—researching, discussing, writing, editing, rewriting, record-keeping, mail-list management, page layout, printing, stuffing, sealing, labeling, sorting, and mailing. And the downside was becoming readily apparent—less time for family rituals and hospitality, less opportunities for talking with the children and involvement in their homeschooling, fewer homemade meals and more junk food, and a house that was getting out of control. I found myself asking the kids not only to do their own work without me, but far too often I expected them to help with my work and to help with the baby.

As I pondered these developments and their impact on my life from the quietness of my teatime chair, the sweet face of my mature oldest daughter came to mind. In just a few short years, she would walk into adulthood, closing forever the door on this precious time of young womanhood. Was I going to have the time to touch her heart for the Lord, to share secrets over mugs of hot tea, to discuss spiritual lessons learned and life decisions to be made? Would I walk by her side through that room of youth and escort her through the door into adulthood, or would I be just an occasional companion as she walked it mostly by herself?

I think, in my heart, I knew where God was taking me, but I had been reluctant to admit it. Clay had already raised the question of whether or not we should continue the newsletter, but I was not convinced. It seemed so obvious, to me anyway, that God had prepared me for this newsletter. All those years of ministry as a single woman, wife, and mother, and all the desires of my heart to be used by God to spiritually encourage other mothers seemed to converge providentially in the *WholeHearted Mother Journal*. It was the fulfillment of a personal dream. And yet this newsletter, which I dearly loved, was threatening to come between me and my family, whom I dearly loved so much more.

I knew in my heart that my arguments to God for keeping the newsletter were just vain attempts to forestall the inevitable. It was just terribly hard to let go of something that I loved, hard to disappoint others, hard to turn off the flow of encouraging letters, hard to give up a longtime dream. And yet, I knew it would be even harder to live with the knowledge that I had chosen the newsletter over my precious husband and children. If I neglected them, my writing and ministry would be a hollow sham. There seemed no other option—I needed to give up the newsletter.

As I was working through this disturbing realization with the Lord, he brought John 6:38 to my mind: "For I have come down from heaven not to do my will but to do the will of him who sent me." It was as if he said to me, "Sally, do you want to do *your* will or *my* will?" Of course, my will was to do the newsletter. But I knew God's will was better—to be fully devoted to my marriage, my children, my home and my God. It wouldn't be enough just to write about it for other mothers—God wanted *me* to be a wholehearted mother!

I could get up from my chair now because God had put the wisdom I sought into my open hands. I could be at peace with the decision because I knew it was right. My family was more important than my newsletter.

ᴥ

I am convinced that the kind of struggle I went through over the *WholeHearted Mother Journal* gets played out in the lives of countless other homeschooling mothers day after day—will we do God's will, or our own? As women, we live in a culture that is constantly telling us that motherhood is a burden and that we can find fulfillment outside the home. We are encouraged to transcend the "limited" role of homemaker and mother to reach for "something higher." Yet, no matter how good that "something higher" might appear to be, it ultimately will leave the one who reaches for it empty-handed if it violates the will of God. The only true, biblical path of blessing for a mother is in reaching out to the children whom God has given to her, to raise and nurture them into godly adults. Fulfillment will come only when a mother is willing to do God's will.

Within the homeschooling movement, some mothers might reach for a newsletter, as I did, or a home business, or a position of leadership, or community involvement, or church activities, or...the list could go on. But if what they are reaching for breaks the firm grip God wants them to have on their children, then they are reaching for the wrong things.

When I told Clay that I was finally willing to let go of my grip on the newsletter, he immediately affirmed my decision. Knowing my desire to minister to women, though, he encouraged me to think instead of writing books and articles as the Lord provided the time. I thought that had settled it, but I guess God knew I needed a little testing to be sure this was a settled conviction in my heart.

When I told one of our employees, who has a wonderful heart for God and for our ministry, I was told in return that I was making a mistake. "You're going to just quit and leave all of those mothers stranded without input?" When I told a dear friend in another city, she said, "A lot of women are going to be very disappointed and let down!" A close friend who lives nearby told me, "God has given you such a special ministry! A lot of moms are going to be really disappointed in you! Are you sure you are not just a quitter?" I didn't want to disappoint anyone, and it was a very difficult decision to make, but I knew in my heart I was doing the right thing.

I felt a bit like Abraham when he had to put his own son, Isaac, on the altar as a sacrifice. He didn't understand why God had asked him to do this thing, but he knew by faith that God would provide. His only response was to obey. In the same way, God had asked me to put the *WholeHearted Mother Journal* on the altar as a sacrifice—to lay down a *good* thing in order to find the *best*. I didn't understand why, but I knew, by faith, that God would provide. And, as I have always found when I sacrifice enjoyable commitments in order to be more available at home, God blessed my decision.

In the months following the decision to let the newsletter die, I felt personally revitalized—my fellowship with the Lord was closer and warmer, my vision as a Christian parent sharper, and my children more precious to me than ever. Through the process of giving up something important for the sake of my children, God has reminded me of some priorities that I don't often associate with homeschooling, but that are inseparable from it in God's design for my life.

Dedication

All throughout the Scriptures, people, places and things are dedicated, or devoted, to the Lord. For God's people, it seems to be a natural, almost instinctual, action to set things aside for God's use. We can also dedicate ourselves, by making our lives completely available to God. In truth, it is simply an act of acknowledging in a special way what is already true—that God is Lord over our lives, our possessions, our families, and all creation.

When we moved into our new house, we dedicated it to the Lord. We gathered our family together and prayed for the house, acknowledging God's ownership of it and asking him to use it for his glory. Each of our children we have dedicated to the Lord, sometimes in church before a body of believers, and sometimes at home in the living room just with our immediate family. We dedicate the books we write to God's use, as this one will be when it comes back from the printer. Although we haven't done so yet, there are some special places that we could have dedicated to God where we experienced great blessing, or special memories, or physical protection.

Confronted with the choice of the newsletter, though, I discovered that I needed to dedicate my life as a mother to the Lord. Without an act of dedication to the task of motherhood that God had set before me, I would always be reaching for that elusive "something else." Once I truly dedicated my "mother's heart" to the Lord, then it would always be my priority, and all other desires for my life would have to fall in line behind it. After my dedication to God as a wife, my dedication to him as a mother would define and guide the direction of my life.

When I read the words of Paul in his letter to the Ephesians, I am struck by God's sovereign control over how I live my life. "For we are God's workmanship, created in Christ Jesus to do good works, which God prepared in advance for us to do." God has already dedicated my life in eternity past to "do good works." His workmanship created me as a mother, and that is the work he has prepared me to do, especially at this time in life when my children are young. How can I ignore that calling on my life and expect to find blessing and fulfillment somewhere else?

In my mind, I see myself as part of a grand tapestry that God is weaving through the lives of his people. My life, and the lives of great men and women throughout redemption history, are the threads God uses as he weaves a picture of truth and reality for the world to see. The thread of my life in these years will be brightly colored and strongly stitched only to the degree that I have dedicated my life to the good work of motherhood that God prepared for me to do in eternity past.

It probably doesn't need to be said, but dedication is not an easy path. Biblical and church history is filled with examples of godly men and women who, having dedicated their lives to their Creator, found themselves persecuted, ostracized, criticized, and rejected. Take a walk through the Hebrews Hall of Faith (chapter 11) and you'll meet some of them. But remember, too, that their threads in God's tapestry of life are the brightest and strongest.

I may not change the world, but perhaps one of my children will. If that is part of the tapestry that I cannot see now (and may not see in my life-time), then those stitches will be added because I have chosen to dedicate my motherhood to God. That is what will make that dedication worth everything that is costs.

Sacrifice

I don't think one can talk about dedication without also talking about sacrifice. Any homeschooling mother who truly dedicates her life to the godly calling of motherhood knows, without having to be convinced, that her decision will require significant, and possibly even life-changing, sacrifices on her part.

You might assume I'm speaking of material or lifestyle kinds of sacrifice, but those are only a small part of the whole. The biggest sacrifice for me has been in the area of relationships and harmony. Once I dedicated my life to biblical motherhood, I very quickly found myself crashing into relational barriers where before there had been none. All of a sudden I was "too committed" to my home and family, and not involved enough in outside activities to give my children a "balanced life." Though I didn't perceive myself as either, some told me I was too "yuppie" and others said I was too "earth mother." Depending on the issue, I was either too conservative, or too liberal; too radical or too lax; too critical or too accepting. I have seen numerous warm relationships cool or die simply because of my convictions about motherhood. That is a difficult sacrifice.

I take some solace, though, in knowing that my sacrifice is like a seed that will produce fruit I cannot even yet see. Jesus said, "I tell you the truth, unless a kernel of wheat falls to the ground and dies, it remains only a single seed. But if it dies, it produces many seeds. The man who loves his life will lose it, while the man who hates his life in this world will keep it for eternal life. Whoever serves me must follow me; and where I am, my servant also will be. My Father will honor the one who serves me." (John 12:24f).

A seed is useless until it is cast into the soil where it will die in order to become something greater—a plant, a flower, a tree. In the same way, my dedication to life at home as a mother is a seed of sacrifice. I give up my own desires and sacrifice my gifts and talents so that new life will come from me. I am buried in the rich soil of housework, homeschooling, character training, disciplining, and all the myriad responsibilities of making a home. To many in my generation, my decision to stay at home is a fruitless sacrifice, a waste of feminine intelligence and abilities. To me, though, it is a small sacrifice if by it I can send my children into the next generation bursting with spiritual life, ready to change their world for Christ. Fruitless? Only by the world's standards. By God's it is a fruitful sacrifice that will yield a harvest of righteousness.

Mary—a dedicated and sacrificial mother

Mary, the mother of Jesus, is a wonderful example to me of dedication and sacrifice. When God asked her to trust him with an incredible responsibility—to conceive the Messiah by the Holy Spirit and to give birth as a virgin—she surely had many things to consider. What would Joseph think? What would her parents and relatives and neighbors say about her pregnancy? Who would believe that an angel had visited her? How could she possibly be a qualified mother for the son of God? Yet she immediately responded, "Be it done to me according to your will!" Her decision was to make God's will her will. She would dedicate her life to God's purposes, even though it would surely mean accepting a life of uncertainty and difficulty. She would sacrifice her life in order to do God's will, even if it meant rejection and loneliness.

The decision to homeschool will, by its nature, create division. To those who choose to put their children in public school, your decision to homeschool is a passive condemnation of their lifestyle. Since homeschooling rejects the educational status quo, it invites criticism and rejection, not just for us as adults but also for our children. Family members, church members, friends, and even strangers will question your decision and scrutinize your life. I am finding that only heart-deep dedication and sacrifice enables me to confidently say, "This is right...this is what God wants me to do...this is worth it." Because I know that doing God's will is worth whatever the cost may be.

ꙮ

I don't know the end of my personal story as yet. I still miss doing my newsletter and hearing from so many like-minded mothers from around the world. There is still a longing in my heart to minister to other women. For now, though, God has asked me to put some of those dreams and desires in the back of my heart. The time is not right, and there are more pressing needs I must attend to as a mother. However, God has a way of reminding me that I have made the right decision.

Soon after we quit the newsletter, God allowed us to move to a wonderful home in Fort Worth. Since it would be physically separated from our business, I hoped it would give me the freedom I desired to focus exclusively on my home and children. After the first few days of unpacking and settling in, Sarah came to me and gave me a tight hug and smiled and said, "Mom, it's so nice to have you back again!" It was like God saying, "See, you did the right thing."

God's will isn't always easy, but it's always right. The fulfillment I enjoyed through the newsletter cannot compare to the joy and peace I experience just being the mother God wants me to be. It's fulfilling to know that I "did the right thing," but that's just the temporal side. Even greater will be my satisfaction when I stand before my Lord and see that my dedication and sacrifice counted for eternity.

❦

Thoughts On the Living Word

If I want to be set apart for God's purposes, then I need to have an intimate knowledge of the God whose purposes I want to serve. The more I fellowship with him through reading his word and through prayer, the more clearly I will begin to be able to know and recognize his will for my life. While other trusted believers may provide some needed wisdom or perspective, God's will is primarily a personal matter discovered by prayer, reflection on his word, and daily obedience. God's will is not something hidden that needs to be found, but something revealed that needs to be done.

John 6:25-40

The Jews were questioning Jesus concerning doing God's will. They wanted a sign and special directions, but Jesus pointed to himself as the answer to their questions. How do you resist God and choose to do your own will instead of submitting to God's will? How do personal desires and cultural expectations keep you from doing God's will? How can you better know the Lord?

John 12:20-28

When Greeks came seeking Jesus, the Lord knew that his time to die for all the world had come. He likened his life to a seed that needed to die. How have you seen the principle of the "seed" at work in your own life, especially as it relates to your role as a mother? What is your "seed," and what "fruit" would it yield? Why do you need to "hate your life" in order to "keep it for eternal life"? What service is God desiring from you that he may "honor" you?

Philippians 2:1-11

Paul exhorts his favorite church to complete his joy in them by being unified in the Lord. Sacrificing your own self-interest, he says, is the way to do that. What is the place of "humility" in motherhood? In what ways is Christ's sacrifice an encouragement for your "attitude" about being a mother? How can you be like Christ as a mother?

John 15:12,13

Jesus teaches his disciples that the highest form of love is self-sacrifice and service that benefits others. In our self-centered, self-indulgent culture, how does this principle come into play in the decision to homeschool? How do you "lay down your life" to love those closest to you? How do you struggle with that principle?

My Thoughts

Thoughts on Living the Word

Several times throughout the year, I will set aside several hours to be alone with the Lord. I'll take my Bible, and a journal to record my thoughts and impressions. I will read and meditate on a passage such as Luke 1:26-38. In my journal, I'll record my thoughts about Mary's decision, and whether I would be able to respond to God the same way. ❧ I also spend time praying for myself, my husband, and my children, asking God to help me know and do his will for me as a woman, wife, and mother. I will also record and confess any areas of sin that are keeping me from being all that God wants me to be. ❧ Finally, I sometimes take a book with me if I have an extended period of time alone. One book that has been especially helpful is *Margin*, by Richard Swenson, M.D.. It helped me think about my life and commitments, see where I was living without margin, and find ways to simplify my life so I could focus on the most important area…my family.

My Life

Personal application: Make a sheet of paper for each child. List out the things in your life that you think each child would say competes with his or her time with you. Choose one thing that you can change or eliminate. Tell each child what you will do.

Family application: Declare a Family Day or Family Weekend and put it on the calendar. Plan in special meals, activities, songs, games, and readings. Spend time looking at family photo albums and pictures. Discuss at meals what makes your family special.

"Women like to make sacrifices in one big piece, to give God something grand, but we can't. Our lives are a mosaic of little things, like putting a rose in a vase on the table."

Ingrid Trobisch
in Heartstrings of Laughter & Love

Chapter Three

Beside Still Waters

The Lord is my shepherd, I shall not be in want.
He makes me lie down in green pastures,
he leads me beside quiet waters,
he restores my soul.

The house was cloaked in quietness and the fading shadows of night that signal the coming dawn. I gingerly tiptoed through the living room, aware that any little noise that broke the silence could awaken a sleeping child. I quickly slipped on my comfortable, broken-in tennis shoes, quietly anticipating the beauty I would find on my private morning walk. It was wildflower season in Texas and I had never seen it so beautiful—pools of deep azure bluebonnets filling up open fields accented by scarlet splashes of Indian Paintbrush. I coaxed open the storm door, managing to stifle its annoying squeak, and sneaked out the final few steps to freedom.

I had barely set foot on the front porch stairs when I heard the soft voice from behind me, "Do you mind if I go with you today, Mom?" It had come from my gentle-spirited, easy-going middle child Joel. I almost never had time alone with him, so I quickly adjusted my expectations for a solitary morning walk, happy to have these few moments together with my firstborn son. "Sure, honey! You go get dressed and I'll wait right here for you." Soon he was back and we headed out into the cool morning.

The road in front of our house was totally deserted, and the brisk morning air raised goose bumps on our arms as the gravel crunched beneath our feet, accentuated by the crisp silence. As the darkness of the last few moments of night slowly retreated, Joel's excited voice broke through the morning silence, "Look at that star, Mommy...the bright one! What is it?" Never in my whole life do I remember seeing the morning star, but it seemed that God had hung it there this morning, radiant against the still black sky, just for our pleasure. I took advantage of a teachable moment to remind Joel that Jesus was called the bright and morning star. Like the real morning star, he is a beautiful light shining in the darkness, a promise of the light of day that is soon to come.

As we stood there enjoying our star, it was as if the Lord wanted us to celebrate that moment with him and his creation. Within minutes, the sky began to glow in shades of pink and soft purple, and soon the beautiful star faded away into a blue expanse as the most beautiful sunrise I can ever remember seeing ushered in the new day. As my sweet boy held my hand and walked with me on that special morning, we marveled together at the creative handiwork of our Creator. The moment was stamped indelibly on my heart. How refreshed we were for the rest of our day.

ঽ

I need regular moments in my life like that morning walk, times of refreshment and restoration that fill up the spiritual well in my heart, which is too often left dry by the spirit-draining hustle and bustle of contemporary life. If I don't take care to keep it filled, I soon find I have no spiritual refreshment to give to those God has put into my life, especially to my always-thirsty children. When I let my well run dry, I am no longer able to be a source of refreshing water to them, or to others. To say it more simply, I cannot keep giving out without taking in.

King David prayed to the Lord, his Shepherd, who "leads me beside quiet waters" (Psalm 23:2). Literally, he said that the Lord would lead him to "waters of resting places." Shepherds knew that not all waters were "restful waters." Some were shallow, warm, stagnant pools. The good ones, though, were deep pools fed by flowing spring waters that kept the surface water cool, refreshing, and restorative. Those waters provided the very best resting places for weary sheep. That is where God leads us to fill our souls.

As a homeschooling mother, keeping my well filled up with restful waters is not always an easy task. I am constantly drawing from it to minister to my children who are always with me, to keep my home-domain in order, to feed and clothe my family, and to be a helper to my husband. In the same way that Jesus often retreated from the needy crowds to spend time alone with God, I realize I need to get away from the needy crowd in my home to be with the Lord, and to draw from his restful waters. He is, after all, the "living water" that will become in those who drink of him "a spring of water welling up to eternal life" (John 4:13,14). Drinking his living water is a spiritual necessity, as necessary for my spiritual health as eating good food is for my physical health. I need to make time to drink of his restful waters to keep my own well filled up!

It is a constant challenge for me to stay filled up so I can be a source of spiritual life to my family. Let me share just a few of the well-filling commitments I am building into my life to make sure I have all the spiritual resources to give that my family needs from me.

I make time for God in my life

As a new Christian in college, I became involved with Campus Crusade for Christ and was trained in their evangelism and discipleship strategy of "win, build and send." I spent many exciting hours sharing my faith with other students, building them in Christ in discipleship groups, and sending them out to do the same. In those early years of my Christian life, I learned a simple truth that has stayed with me all through my adult life: I cannot give out what I have not taken in. If I wanted to help others grow in Christ, I needed to be growing in Christ. And the single most reliable indicator if that is happening in my life is whether or not I am spending personal time with God every day.

I have added a husband and four children to my life since those days, but that simple truth has lost none of its strength. When I was in college, I spent only a few hours a week with my "disciples," and (I can admit it now) I could get by in a pinch on a spiritual tank running low. Now, though, my "disciples" are with me 24 hours a day, every day, and there is no hiding it when I am spiritually depleted. And it only gets worse when new babies, illnesses, moves, and other crises hit, and any extra time in my schedule is used up on meeting needs and getting things done. It doesn't take long to find myself running on empty.

Unless I want my spirit to be as dissipated as my calendar, though, I know I have to make time to be with God—to read the Bible, to pray, to worship God in my spirit, to sing songs of praise. If I'm not taking in, I'll have nothing to give out, much less to sustain my spirit through the times when I most need to live by faith. I have seen that my life almost always gets out of balance in some way when I don't make time for God. God's word, though, will revive my soul (Ps. 19:7), giving me the new life in him I need for each new day.

Even though my need for time with God grows stronger every year, it seems more and more difficult to find the time I need. One would think God would have built in the time in relation to the need, but apparently it doesn't work that way. The greater my need has become for God, the greater has become my need to work hard to make time in my life for him. It rarely happens by accident. Perhaps God knows that it will make that time all the more precious if it is hard to come by.

The "easiest" way I have found to make time is to follow the advice of Ben Franklin, "early to bed and early to rise." If I can get in bed a little earlier, I can get up a little earlier for a quiet time. As many times as not, though, I find myself sharing my quiet morning space with one or more radar-eared children. That is why I sometimes leave the house early and go somewhere for coffee and quiet time. When I'm not consistent in the early-to-bed part, I have to make time during the later-in-the-day part to get in a few devotional minutes when the baby is napping and the children are reading.

The key is my own sense of need. If I listen to the needs of my spirit, I will find a way to make the time to get alone with God. You need to determine when you can best be alone with God and organize your life to make sure it happens.

I make time for myself in my life

When I first went overseas as a missionary with Campus Crusade, I received some good advice from my director. It sounded more like Shakespeare's counsel, "to thine own self be true," than purely biblical counsel, but it proved to be just as helpful to this young single woman moving into Poland in 1977. He said that each person, if they are going to last in the mission field, needs to look at their personality and determine what things they need in their lives to keep going. For one it might be certain foods, for another favorite music or books, for another familiar furniture, for another regular contact with home. For me, it was having a home environment that was warm and pleasant.

My understanding of my God-given personality has deepened considerably since then, especially as I have added the roles of wife and mother to my life's experience. God made me a certain way, with preferences for how I think, make decisions, order my life, and relate to others. For instance, I know that I am a more reflective, or introverted, personality, rather than more active, or extraverted. When I was younger, I mistakenly thought that introverted meant "shy." Now I understand it as indicating that my mental energies are focused internally, on thoughts and ideas, rather than externally, on people and activities. By nature, I prefer a reflective lifestyle as opposed to an active one.

That helps me understand why, even though I love ministering to and influencing people, I get physically and emotionally drained speaking at weekend seminars. All of my energy has to be focused outwardly, which is not natural to my personality. It's no wonder that as soon as the workshop is over I feel a deep need to get away and be by myself. I need reflective time alone to refill my spiritual well.

It also helps me understand why I need regular time away from my children. Homeschooling is not an introverted lifestyle. Four little people want my attention every moment of the day, and there are other big ones standing in line when they are through with me! Since it is impossible to find a place or the time to be alone in a house full of people, I have learned to be creative.

There is a wonderful French bakery about ten minutes from my home that has become my private getaway. Just the atmosphere ministers to my soul—French-roasted coffee, brick-oven baked European breads, a fresh-cut flower on each wooden table, Baroque music in the background. It is so reminiscent of the Viennese coffeehouses that Clay and I frequented during our years there. If I can go there even for just an hour in the early morning, by myself, and have my own quiche and coffee without anyone begging for a taste, I come home a totally different person. I am newly invigorated and ready for the active life of running after my four always-on-the-go, chattering little squirrels I call my children.

On rare occasions of personal crisis, I have needed an extended time alone. Several years ago, I suffered a serious miscarriage during which I lost a large amount of blood leaving me very anemic. While I was recovering, my father became ill and died. I was already drained from starting a new homeschool group with classes for 120 children and a Bible study for the mothers, and from a broken relationship with another couple at church. I was exhausted physically, emotionally, and spiritually. To give me some time to recuperate, Clay offered to take the children home to Texas to visit their grandmother for two weeks. I definitely needed their time away.

I had in mind that while they were gone I would clean and organize the house, get the homeschooling files in shape, read a book or two about homeschooling to get me refreshed and re-motivated, and spend some extended time with the Lord. Instead, I slept a lot, ate my favorite foods, went out to restaurants with my mother who flew in to visit me, met a couple of friends for lunch, watched some old movies, and spent some casual time reading my Bible. I accomplished very little while everyone was gone, but when they returned I was refreshed, rejuvenated, and ready to get back to real life again. I just needed some physical, emotional, and spiritual rest.

Whatever personality God has given to you, be sure you give yourself the time to be refreshed in a way that is right for you. There is no single, one-size-fits-all formula for how and where that happens for everybody, but you need enough time with yourself to determine how and where it will happen for you.

I make time for beauty in my life

Throughout our marriage, Clay and I have made it a habit to "memorialize" special events in our lives with something beautiful. On our honeymoon, we purchased a small pressed flower arrangement mounted between two pieces of glass that stood on attached legs. It has stayed with us all these years to remind us of God's love and care for us in our marriage verse, "Observe how the lilies of the field grow; they do not toil nor do they spin, yet I say to you that even Solomon in all of his glory did not clothe himself like one of these" (Matt. 6:28-29, NASB).

Our ability to appreciate beauty is a distinctive mark of God's image within us, much like our ability to use language. God made us to enjoy and benefit from beauty, whether in the things he created or in the things we create. In contrast to the common and crass things of this world which have a negative effect on our spirits, we are naturally drawn to and find pleasure in expressions of beauty—majestic mountains, burning sunsets, starry heavens, captivating paintings, inspiring music, moving poetry. Beauty brings us closer to the Creator, whose very nature and presence is the ultimate expression of beauty.

I have filled my home with expressions of beauty because I need to stay in touch with that part of God's image within me. It is a reminder to me in the midst of so much that is common and dull that I live in a world created by a God of unadulterated beauty and unlimited creativity. Beautiful pictures on the walls, a creative centerpiece, a roaring fire, a bright spray of flowers, flickering candlelight at dinner, creative calligraphy, lovely books, classical music—all are ways that I can bring beauty into my home.

Even a small touch of beauty can minister to my spirit. Recently, a cranky washer died in the middle of the night. We were greeted that morning by two inches of water covering the kitchen and living room floors. Every towel in the house was thrown into action mopping up the kitchen, and the living room soon became a disaster area with stuff and furniture piled in the center of the room. It was a mess.

At the end of that day, a sweet friend brought me a small pot of beautiful petit roses. As I endured the mess in succeeding weeks, I drew pleasure from those lovely roses each time I passed them. In spite of the messes surrounding them, I was refreshed by their beauty and loveliness.

I have found two keys that unlock the ministry of beauty in my home: to be creative in using beauty, and to take the time to admire it. To have some tea is one thing; to have a tea time with a creatively set table, candles, music, and a beautiful book is quite another. A cup of tea may temporarily satisfy the palate, but a tea time can satisfy the soul if you take the time to unlock the beauty that is possible there.

Beauty keeps my spirit refreshed. Without it, my spirit becomes dull and lifeless; with it, I am invigorated and encouraged. God has certainly made beauty a priority in his universe, so I can imitate him by making room for beauty in my home.

I make time for friends in my life

When I lived in Nashville, a number of us moms would get together for a Mom's Night Out. Sometimes, I was tempted just to stay home, but went anyway. Someone usually came to the meeting saying, "I had the worst day in the world. You just won't believe what my kids did today!" Another friend would chime in with her stresses, which sounded even worse. Before long, in the midst of sharing our war stories with one another, we would be laughing at each other's dilemmas, commiserating and identifying with each other's struggles, and sharing scriptures and stories. We rarely solved any major problems or relieved any heavy burdens, but just knowing that we were comrades in a common battle allowed us to leave feeling refreshed and encouraged.

That group taught me an important lesson about my needs. In Ecclesiastes 4:9, the Teacher says, "Two are better than one because they have a good return for their labor. For if either of them falls, the one will lift up his companion. But woe to the one who falls when there is not another to lift him up" (NSAB). Many other scriptures underscore this simple truth, that God made us to need one other and to be accountable to one other. When we are alone, without input from another like-minded person, we can lose objectivity and begin to feel isolated. That is especially true for me as a homeschooling mother. When I spend so much time at home with my children, I need the support and encouragement of other homeschooling mothers to keep me going.

Because we have moved so often, I have been without friendships quite a bit. I am committed, though, to staying in touch regularly with several far-away close friends. They provide a continuity of friendship, counsel, and input that I have missed because of our moves, even though we relate only by phone, mail, and email. When I find myself without a close group of friends, I also have learned to let certain newsletters, books by women I admire, and seminars for women and mothers become a kind of temporary support system for myself until God brings new friends along. Clay, of course, is my best friend, but I believe women need other women friends, especially for this journey of Christian motherhood. That is why, I think, God instructs older women to teach the younger.

I try to open my home once or twice a month for a fellowship for moms. It has been a well-spring of encouragement for me and has been the basis for many developing friendships with women I otherwise would never have known. I recently started a mother-daughter Bible study. I want Sarah, too, to see how God blesses us through friendships, especially when we meet and share around his word. How sweet it is to see her sharing from her own heart what she is learning about from life, the Lord, and her own struggles, and to see other girls also beginning to respond.

When I spend time beside the restful waters with my Lord, it is not just because I selfishly need to be refreshed. Rather, it is because my children need to refreshed, and my husband, and my neighbors, and my friends, and the world. I am here to live, not for myself, but for Jesus. He is the living water who wants to live in me, and wants me to let his life flow through my own, and into the lives of others around me.

Whatever my year ahead may hold, if I am going to be a spring of refreshing water to my family, it will be only because I have kept my own well filled with living water. I want to be to them like that glorious morning walk with Joel was to me. I want to be a channel of God's grace so that when they are with me they are being touched in some small way by the eternal. I may not always be as glorious as a morning sunrise, but I am a part of God's creation, too, and I can shine with God's glory within my family...if I am full of his glory to begin with. I can give out only as much as I take in. But there is always enough beside the restful waters where he leads me.

Thoughts On the Living Word

In a goal-driven culture such as ours, the concepts of rest and restoration are lost in the frenzied pace of our constant activity and never-an-empty-calendar-space lives. Even Sunday, God's "day of rest," can become a harried holy day of church services and events from morning to evening. Yet God knows our bodies and spirits need physical rest in order to be spiritually restored. He has built it into our natures, and even into the rhythm of creation. As a homeschooling mother, I have learned the absolute necessity of rest. Without it, I am vulnerable and tired; with it, I am capable and strong. Okay, so maybe I'm still a little tired, but I know I have enough strength and reserve to make it. And that makes all the difference.

Psalm 23

David meditates on the loving leadership of God, his Shepherd and King. How does God make you like down in "green pastures" and lead you to "quiet waters"? What are they like, and how does he restore your soul there? Do you ever resist his efforts to make you lie down, or to drink of his waters? How and why?

Psalm 19:7-11

David reflects on God's general revelation of himself in nature, and his special revelation of himself in his word, the Law. How does the "law of the Lord" revive your soul? What other life-nurturing effects does God's word bring about? What have you done recently to let the word of God revive you? When you are revived, what difference does it make in your mothering?

Ecclesiastes 4:9-11

The writer of Ecclesiastes contemplates the obvious value of companions. Does reading this passage bring anyone to mind who is like that in your life? Are you that kind of friend to someone else? Consider who might become a supportive friend to you and your family.

Matthew 6:31-34

Jesus, in his Sermon on the Mount, admonishes his listeners to stop worrying about their lives because God will provide what is needed. Are you more like the "pagans" who "run after" what they need, or like the "seeker" who rests in God? If you stopped worrying about tomorrow, what difference would it make in your life? Would you be able to "seek first his kingdom and his righteousness" more?

My Thoughts

Thoughts on Living the Word

I have found that it is fundamental to my mental health for me to find fifteen minutes sometime during the day for a one-woman tea time. Reading from a favorite book or magazine with a good cup of tea relaxes and refreshes me somehow. The kids know that during that time I want to be alone. ❧ I will regularly look for something new I can do to or obtain for my home that will beautify it or enhance the environment, even if it is just a very small thing or project. I might find a new CD of classical or instrumental music, buy a potted flower for my kitchen, rearrange the fireplace mantle with new candlesticks and candles, or hang a new picture in the den. ❧ To find the kind of fellowship with other wholehearted mothers that I desired, I went so far as to start a monthly Mom's Night Out at our house. I have also arranged discussion groups, Bible studies, and teas that brought other likeminded mothers into my home. I have found the fellowship has always been worth the small cost of being the hostess.

My Life

Personal application: In your quiet time, ask God to show you a verse that is especially refreshing to you. Set aside a time when you can go shopping alone. Look for something beautiful or lovely that will be a visual reminder to you of that verse.

Family application: Plan a "formal" tea party for your children. Invite several of their friends. Plan to use your best table settings, and have classical music, candles, and such. Of course, plan a child-pleasing desert or some tasty pastries. Have everyone "dress up" for the occasion.

Summer ~ Season *of* Response

Summer

Thoughts on Response
Ten Years Later

A glorious July summer day was upon me as I watched the gusty mountain breezes make swaying giants of the tall pines outside my window. With a deep sense of leisure, I enjoyed this small dance of creation as I sipped my last drop of morning tea. I had enjoyed a rare, uninterrupted morning quiet time in which I actually had a chance to read, look out the window, and ponder over a new book I had received from a friend. I felt ready now to tackle my waiting agenda, and was set to plan the rest of my month. I had a lot of work to accomplish and I could feel its weight heavy on my shoulders.

For two months, while older siblings were out of town, we were once again a two-child household. I had almost forgotten how much easier life is with just two at home. I had never had my younger two children entirely alone, and I appreciated this peaceful season with fewer needs to meet. I was also really enjoying the personality and antics of my younger two, who were presently free to claim my undivided attention.

But I also had much to do this summer by way of plans: clean out the bulging closets from clothes (some that were never worn), slug through the stacks of papers that had mounted up on my desk during the busy spring (which had been filled with ministry and travel), and finish Joy's math for the year. Last, but far from least, I needed to finish the longest book I had yet proposed to write, which was due by September. I felt my head whirling slightly with all this ahead, and still whirling a bit from the plethora of graduation parties and a wedding in our home for a friend just behind us. Clay was also helping me to start two new blogs which brought even more writing my way. I needed this day to plan, and I needed to write. I had barely begun work on the book, but for one day Joy was out playing with a friend, so I had to make my time count when the kids were out of the house. It was a rare thing indeed for everyone to be so occupied.

And then came the knock on my door. In response to my hesitant, "Come in," Nathan poked his head inside my door.

Nathan, at 18, had been busy all summer with his many friends who had just finished the high school portion of their lives. His group of boys had designated every single day of the summer as their last chance to celebrate and make memories before they all went to various schools, work opportunities, and internships in the fall. As they banged in and out of the door almost daily, they reminded me of a hysterically bouncy and playful set of puppies frolicking, nipping, and growling at each other. They lived in endless circles of laughter, eating, talking, and "going somewhere" when anyone had free time—not one moment was lost! Nathan worked as a pizza delivery boy in between and took the occasional weekend job for a local marketing company. I had learned to give up my expectations of seeing him very much in this busy season of life.

"Hey, Mom, my friends are all busy today and I don't have to work until tomorrow. How about you and I go out to lunch together today or go out for coffee or something since I don't have any definite plans yet!"

My mind immediately began to calculate what it "cost" me to change my plans and give them all up for the spur of the moment whims of my appealing son. I was so late getting this book written, there were just two more weeks of free time before I had to travel again, and Sarah and Joel would be back soon. I decided not even to contemplate the crammed agenda of the coming fall. Instead, I just looked up and smiled.

"Let me take care of a few details and make a couple of phone calls, and then my day belongs to you," I answered back with as much enthusiasm as I could muster.

"Great!" he beamed back. "And I know you would just love to make me a piece of your cinnamon toast and a cup of tea if you are in the kitchen and I would love it too. How 'bout I be your little boy today?"

Nathan had always been a charmer and he knew he could get me to do almost anything for him these days. I had made a decision that he and Joy would be highest priority to me this summer, whatever it took. After living through the expanding lives of Sarah and Joel, I knew that the window of opportunity for building my values, messages, and love for God into the lives of my two youngest children would soon close. So, when an opportunity arose to speak into Nathan's heart, I knew without hesitation to grab it!

As I made his very late breakfast of tea and toast, I began to pray and search in my mind for ideas to make this day an especially memorable one. Maybe, if I bribed him with a lunch date, he would be willing to go on a short, strategic hike with me. My idea was beginning to come together as well as if it had been planned for months.

I knew intuitively that someone would probably call Nathan with an activity or get-together by mid-afternoon, so I planned my time well. As he munched and sipped, I suggested jumping in the car, going to Barnes & Noble for a quick look at some books, magazines, and music, followed by lunch at his favorite restaurant. Then I added, "And I do have one more place I want to take you that will be a little of a surprise and won't take too long. OK?"

With an offer of some of his favorite activities, Nathan agreed to my plan. We climbed into his car and took off down the freeway, with him driving energetically as boys his age do, and music blaring just beyond the levels of my noise comfort zone. But I was delighted to have this time to invest in a memory. After musing at the bookstore, and catching up on thoughts and happenings over lunch, we were ready to end our time with my planned adventure.

"Drive to Glen Eyrie Castle," I directed, knowing he would know the way. Having spoiled him for a couple of hours, I had earned my right to speak into his life. "I want to show you something I don't think you have ever seen and I promise it won't take long."

Glen Eyrie is the beautiful headquarters and conference center of The Navigators, an international discipleship ministry. The "Castle" was built by General William Palmer, the founder of Colorado Springs, for his wife on one of the choicest foothills properties in the region surrounded by pines and red rock outcroppings. He spared no expense in building the Castle, bringing in materials and interior décor from all over the world. But like so many other "Gilded Age" mansions, it passed out of the family and through several owners. In 1951, God enabled Dawson Trotman to purchase the Castle and surrounding property for The Navigators.

"You know, Mom," said my restless boy. "I've pretty much hiked every part of the grounds and seen everything the Glen has to offer. And remember, I do need to get home to finish some of the work I planned on doing."

"You will be glad that we did this. I promise!" I assured Nathan as we drove through the entrance gate. As I directed him to a back parking lot near one of the staff cottages, I told him that we were going to take a short hike and end up at a place that had become special to me.

Walking up the red dirt trail in the gentle sun of a perfect mountain day, we slowly wound around the green slopes, always climbing, and chatting about memories of our family stays at the Glen in previous years. Finally, we crested the hill and Nathan saw a bench perched on the pine-covered hillside. It peered over a beautiful vista of mountains, trees, skies, and the spire of the Glen Eyrie Castle, nestled in the glen below. As we came upon the sitting area, there on the ground were the tombstones of Dawson Trotman and his wife Lila, who died within a year of one another. We caught our breath and sat down.

"I brought you here because it is a favorite place of mine to pray," I began, as the wind cooled us off. "Dawson Trotman started this ministry as an outreach to young military men who desperately needed to know the love and grace of God. Through his ministry thousands of young adults and college students became Christians and learned how to study the Bible and how to have a ministry to others. He was just a normal man who trusted God to do great things."

As I warmed up to my story, I went on to recount for Nathan the history of how Dawson, a young man of God, had a vision for Glen Eyrie as a place to teach and train Christians from all over the world, and how he dedicated his life to "knowing God and making God known" through the ministry of The Navigators. But he did more than give his life spiritually for others, I told Nathan, he also gave his life physically. Not long after moving to Glen Eyrie, Dawson was on a trip to New York to visit friends. On a water skiing outing, a young woman who couldn't swim was thrown into the lake. Dawson went in after her, holding her head above water until she was safe again in the boat, but before the others could reach him, he went under and drowned. He gave his life serving and saving others.

"Dawson Trotman was a great man.," I said to Nathan, "and I think that God is making you into a great man, too. I'm praying that, just like he did with Dawson, he'll use you to influence many people for Christ. I don't know exactly how he'll do that yet, but I am confident he will." I touched his hand and said, "I would like to dedicate your life to the Lord here today, in prayer. You are on the brink of venturing out into the world to discover the work God created you to do. But before I do, I want to tell you some of the special and unique qualities I see in your life that I appreciate."

I took the next few moments to remind Nathan of his many good qualities and skills—his fun personality and ease with people, his artistic and creative skills, his sketches and photographs, his ability to be such a good friend, his music, and his heart for the Lord and desire to serve him. "I can't wait to see what God does in your life," I ended. "Can we pray together to commit your life, dreams, desires for a wife, and your future work and ministry to the Lord?"

Nathan and I held hands and prayed together, yielding his life symbolically on this mountaintop to the Lord. It was one of those poignant, memorable moments that I will never forget. But it happened only because I took an opportunity to be with him, and turned it into a moment to celebrate him and to give his life to God. Memory accomplished!

As we hiked back to the car, we talked and giggled, and discussed lots of "stuff" that came easily to our minds. But my heart was full knowing that whatever was ahead, we had together committed his life into God's hands, and that Nathan had let me, one more time, be a voice of truth in his life.

On the drive back home, Nathan said quite out of the blue, "Mom, why don't you make a steak dinner for my boys and spoil them. Then maybe you could tell them some of what you've told me, about their futures and loving God and being committed to really eternal things. Would you do that for me?"

I said a breathless, bright-eyed "Yes!" I could hardly imagine that my 18 year-old would be willing to expose his own best buds to his mother's impassioned thoughts, but the fact that it was his idea, not mine, spoke loudly of his own good heart. I was thrilled and honored.

Several weeks later, we did just that. There was an abundance of laughter, fun, and celebration as the boys all feasted on grilled steak and all the fixings. When they were full of food, we moved onto the couches where I shared with them. To a chorus of deep chuckles, I complemented Nathan on choosing the handsomest, smartest, best boys he could find to be his friends. I let them know how glad we were to know them, and that I wanted to encourage them about their journey ahead. I simply shared five foundational verses with them that I thought were biblical priorities on which they should build the foundations of their lives.

How amazed I was as they patiently looked up the Bible verses and chatted with me about what they meant to them. We prayed all together and I dedicated each boy into God's hands, and asked him to guide them, bless them, and watch over them. As I left soon after that, each young man hugged me a hearty goodbye. They were all leaving home in the next few days, and I might not see them again for a while, but I left feeling complete.

ᨀ

There is a summer season of life in which the lives and hearts of my children are open to the sowing of much seed. It is a season in which God wants me to be ready to respond to their open hearts, and to make the most of each moment. It is a time when God asks me to cultivate, sow into, and water the gardens of my children's hearts in a season of growing.

From the time a toddler can understand language until the time when middle school-aged children begin to move toward maturity, there are seasons when their hearts are open and ready for planting seeds which will bear future fruit of spiritual truth, emotional health, moral standards, educational excellence, and general well being. These are the times in which I have to take every opportunity to cultivate the ground of my children's hearts in order for them to be able to take in the seeds of right-eousness that God has prepared me to plant there.

There is still time for planting in the high school and college years, but the days are shorter then. This season is meant for children to mature, to begin the owning of their own lives and convictions. Other voices begin to speak into their lives. The time of seed-sowing in the life of a child is one that must be treasured and used well, because it will come to a sudden end as the seeds grow to full fruit and the time for the harvest has come.

The season of planting is not forever; it is a gift of time granted for a single, fleeting season. But what precious time. I have come to understand that it really will determine the future harvest in the lives of my children. The outcome of my children's souls depends in large part upon how well I plant the seeds of love, righteousness, and deep heart training while I have the time. The great stories of heroic people that I can sow in their minds, the words of life and biblical instruction, the times of character development, and generous encouragement and daily affection will yield the harvest of a rich young soul. I think that in many ways the heart of the mother's soul is reflected in the soul harvest of her children. What we sow, we will indeed also reap.

How important it is then, that I take every opportunity to be a skillful and wise farmer of the souls of my children. I must faithfully and generously work the ground of my children's hearts, plant seeds of righteousness, and water those seeds with my love and prayers, because the season of harvest is ahead, when there will be no more time to plant. And it will come sooner and more quickly than I expect.

But it will be a season of plentiful celebration if I have planted well. If I have lived daily in touch with my heavenly Father, and I have responded to my children as they have passed through their own seasons, then I can be confident that God will work in my children's hearts and lives. If I want to see a harvest in their souls, they will need to see me responding to God. It is what God has called me to do.

❦

Summer

Rejoice in the Lord always, I will say it again:
Rejoice! Let your gentleness be evident to all.
The Lord is near.

Do not be anxious about anything, but in
everything, by prayer and petition, with
thanksgiving, present your requests to God.

And the peace of God, which transcends all
understanding, will guard your hearts and
your minds in Christ Jesus.

Philippians 4:4-7

"The process of shaping the child...shapes also the mother herself. Reverence for her sacred burden calls her to all that is pure and good, that she may teach primarily by her own humble, daily example."

Elizabeth Elliot
The Shaping of a Christian Family

Chapter Four

Building Your House

The wise woman builds her house, but with
her own hands the foolish one tears her down.

S arah sits cross-legged across from me on our king-sized bed, sipping a cup of hot tea, obviously savoring the adultness of the moment. Tonight, we'll read a chapter from *Beautiful Girlhood*, a lovely book by Mabel Hale from 1922. We'll talk about it, turning topics that might seem mundane to other girls in contemporary culture into matters of serious discussion. Chapters on propriety, purity, beauty, and femininity are all starting points that take us on a variety of mother-daughter discussion trails.

On other nights like this one we might study the Bible together, or share secrets with a whisper, or just giggle a lot. It's our Monday night "girl talk," a special time when we meet privately in my bedroom, just Sarah and me. Although it is supposed to be mostly for Sarah, I sometimes can't help but wonder if the greater impact is on me. As I try to distill, in just a few words, a lifetime of reflection and experience, the Spirit of God reminds me of my responsibility to "redeem the time" with my children, to "make the most of every opportunity."

As I look at my precious thirteen year-old firstborn, with the first blush of womanhood beginning to show in her spirit and body, I realize there won't be enough Monday nights to tell her all I want her to know. They will pass all too quickly in the torrent of time that sweeps away the weeks, months, and years in a rush of living. When we pull away from the current onto our little Monday night island, though, I catch sight of the changes that I have missed in the rush. I see her slowly shedding the cloak of childhood, tentatively trying on the mantle of young adulthood, and I realize just how short my time with her is. All too soon, we'll sit on this bed and talk, not just as mother and daughter, but as two grown women.

I know I'll never be completely ready for that time, but I pray with all my heart that Sarah will be. I look at the world I am preparing her to enter and I shudder at the distortions and perversions of true femininity that will vie for my little girl's heart, mind and soul. Even now, cartoon caricatures of femininity are a child's-eye preview of what awaits—rebellious Ariels, non-conformist Belles, independent Jasmines, sensual Pocahontases. These, and so much worse, are the models now for other girls like Sarah who, for the most part, will not sit on their mothers' beds and talk of God's eternal design for men and women. Her adult world will be full of them.

And following close on Sarah's heels are two boys who will be wanting to become men. Clay will shape their ideas and ideals of masculinity, but God has given me tremendous influence over their lives as a mother. How I handle their transitions to manhood, and the lifelong connections of mother and son, will have a profound influence on the shape and direction of their lives. And then, when most other mothers I know will be facing the "empty nest," sweet little Joy will just be entering young womanhood, just as her older sister Sarah is now. And I'll do it all over once again.

So, I find myself praying more than normal after my Monday nights with Sarah. The words of the proverb ring in my heart: "The wise woman builds her house, but with her own hands the foolish one tears hers down." They set my heart to questioning my own efforts to build the house God has given me. What am I doing? Is it enough? Am I building my house or, God forbid, tearing it down? Is the foundation strong? Will the house stand? Do I know what to do with the few short years God puts these children under my care and influence? Will I be the wise woman? In Sarah's case, will she accept the mantle of biblical womanhood as she becomes a woman, wife, and mother? Will she imitate my life? Will she pick up where I leave off?

❧

I wrestle daily, it seems, with what it means to be the "wise woman" mentioned in Proverbs. When I read that passage, I really want to know what it means for her to "build her house." Not very much is said about it, so I'm left to fill in the blanks. Certainly, there are many other practical scriptures I can turn to for principles on family building, but this proverb assumes that the reader understands what it means. Perhaps it appeals to the instinctual nature of a woman to do what God has already designed into her nature to do—build a home and rule over her domain. That, I believe, is what defines the difference between the wise and the foolish woman—one is building, the other is not. One is in touch with God's design for her life, one is not. And, if I read correctly between the lines of the Hebrew poetry, if I am not building, then I am tearing down. And that would be a foolish thing to do.

In Proverbs 24:3,4, the house is "built" by wisdom, "established" through understanding, and "filled" with beauty through knowledge. I like to think of this proverb as describing how the wise woman of 14:1 furnishes the house she is building. I want my house to be strong, but I also want it to be a place full of life and truth. A house that is filled with "rare and beautiful treasures" will satisfy the soul as well as be a place of safety and refuge. That is what I want my house to be for my children.

So, I choose to build, and to keep building. That is what God designed me, as a woman, to do. And despite the sometimes unrelenting hardships and difficulties that come with family-building, God has promised ample blessings and rewards for any parent who chooses to reach for the goal of building a biblical home and family. I realize that neither I, nor any other woman, will ever fully attain to that goal. But it is in the day-to-day process of *reaching* for it—of doing the building—that I have found my greatest fulfillment as a mother, and as a woman.

Three general principles that I want to share with you will help you get started, or keep going, with building your home. These are the steps of a "wise woman," for it is in the process of building that you will grow in wisdom.

Start building with a good plan

If you try to build a real house without a plan, you probably won't build for very long. The lines you thought were straight will be crooked, nothing will fit together the way you thought it would, and the plans you were sure would work won't. Even if it does get built, it won't stand long because uneven walls and a shaky foundation will not withstand even a minimal amount of stress from the outside. In the end you will probably end up tearing down the bricks and boards and starting over. All your hard work would be in vain.

We have counseled countless people in our more than twenty years of ministry. Almost without exception, individuals who came to us with counseling needs of one sort or another grew up in homes fractured by sin and discord of one kind or another. In most cases, the experience of growing up in a "dysfunctional family" has been the norm rather than the exception. Even though I can speak only from second-hand knowledge of what their homes may have been like, I feel confident about one thing that can be said of every one of them—their mothers did not set out with a plan to purposely "tear down" their homes. No matter how poorly their children turned out, these women did not lay out a plan for being a less-than-effective mother. And yet, from what we could tell from the lives of their grown children, their mothers may as well have made such a plan. What is even more clear from their children's lives, though, is that these mothers had no plan for "building." Though they had not planned to "tear down" their homes, neither had they planned to "build" them. And without a proven plan for building their homes and families, they simply tore them down by default.

On the other hand, when we meet individuals or couples whose lives we are drawn to and admire, we are always curious to find out who or what influenced them the most as believers. We are never surprised if we hear that they grew up in Christian homes where the parents had a clear sense of God's design for family. In so many cases, it is clear that the mother had the vision of the "wise woman" who had a plan for building her home. It mattered little whether it was a complex or simple plan, or what kind of personality she had, or what kind of house they lived in. What mattered is that she knew what she wanted to accomplish in her children's lives, and she had a plan for making that happen. She was committed to building her house.

If you want your children to become godly adults, the planning must start now, while they are still young. Begin to define your vision for your children: How can I develop their character? How will I instruct them in biblical truth? How will I train them in righteousness and morality? How can I inspire them with a biblical vision for life? How will I teach them to serve others? How will I strengthen their relationships with others and the Lord? What traditions should we celebrate to enhance our life messages? What is the best education for my children? How will I order our home routines and lifestyle? And on and on.

The more clearly you define your vision for your children, and the more specific your plan for carrying out that vision, the more confident you will become at the daily process of building your home. If your plan is based on clear biblical principles, you won't be easily swayed by the conflicting voices of other opinions that will try to convince you that you are not doing it right. And if you are secure in your vision and plan, your children will be more secure because of your confidence. So, start with a good plan. Know where you want to go with your family, and what you want your children to become, and start building. That's how God planned it.

Build on a strong foundation

When I was a young mother, I had very high ideals for my children's behavior and values. My mind was clouded by visions of children who behaved properly in all situations, enthusiastically loved whatever I loved, naturally desired and enjoyed fine art and music, and were always eager to learn.

After nearly fourteen years of motherhood, reality has cleared my vision. I've discovered that ideals are much less "fixed" than I once thought. More times than I care to admit, I have found myself re-examining ideals I once would have called non-negotiable. Many times my ideals turn out to be nothing more than my own opinions blown out of proportion by overzealous expections. Even biblical convictions can balloon up to be much more imposing than God intended them to be. However, I've also discovered that many (hopefully most) of my ideals have eternal significance and weight. What I built on in the beginning has proven a strong and reliable foundation.

The key to building a strong home, I have found, is identifying those foundational ideals that have eternal weight, and concentrating my building time on those. That means that the process of re-examination is critical to the process of building my home. As my walk with the Lord becomes more mature and my understanding of his word more complete, it is a sign of spiritual health and vitality for convictions to mature and grow as well. That is what keeps the foundation strong, and the stronger the foundation that I build upon, the more stable the home will be.

For example, two foundational principles of the Christian life have become increasingly important to me that I want to pass along to my children: to love God and to love people (Mat. 22:37-40). Jesus said that "all the Law and the Prophets hang on these two commandments." In other words, this was how Jesus defined maturity.

As much as I want my children to be mature, every day is a fresh reminder to me that I cannot force them to become mature. However, even though I cannot always make them behave the way I would like them to, I can always do what Jesus did—speak to their hearts. It is hard to envision Jesus laying down the law and demanding obedience of my children. I imagine Jesus would look beyond the unacceptable and immature behavior, and gently and lovingly address the thoughts and motivations of their hearts. Were they loving God? Were they loving people? In the end, all of my parental laws and prophetic exhortings hang on these two commands!

If my children are misbehaving, I can make them stop. Whether with a strong rebuke, an angry stare, a stern tone of voice, a distasteful consequence, or more severe measures, I have the authority and power to put an end to their misdeeds. It's not that difficult to control external behavior. It is much more difficult, though, to look beyond the behavior and address the heart issues behind it. And at the very heart of all human behavior (which includes young humans) is our love for God and our love for others. Those are the foundational issues that should be first on my mind, not just their immature behavior.

But it's not enough for my children just to hear me talk to them about loving God and loving people, they also must see me doing it. God will be real to them only if he is real to me. Sunday School and Bible clubs may reinforce what I am doing at home, but children imitate and become what they see in their parents. In the same way, my children will not grow in maturity because I have taught them the right things, read them the best books, or used the right curriculum. They will mature because I have shaped their hearts to love God and to love people.

There are other foundational Christian truths and values that I plan to instill in my children, such as dependence upon God's word, living by faith, walking in the Spirit, grace and freedom, integrity and others. If I can pour them into their lives for a solid, strong foundation, then I know that whatever else I, or they, build on top of it will stand strong. The stronger the foundation, the stronger the home.

Count the cost to build

Clay and I have lived this principle in real life. We have "built" two houses, both of which cost more, both in time and money, than we had anticipated. We know by the hard road of experience that it pays to count the cost before you begin to build.

When you're talking about building your family, it is even more essential to count the cost. You do so to be sure you are willing to pay the price of building, to finish what you begin (Lk. 14:28f). There is a price to pay for building your home and family according to God's plan, and the cost is especially high for the homeschooling mother.

There is the physical cost of weariness from teaching and caring for children with constant needs, from doing housework and laundry, from making countless meals, from picking up the same toys over and over again. There is the emotional cost of always being expected to give affection and attention to ever-present children, of directing their education, of training their spirits and disciplining them, of being available to them for what seems like 24 hours a day, 365 days a year. There is the personal cost of giving up personal expectations, of sacrificing personal "rights" for the benefit of the children, of accepting the limitations of time, of often choosing to live and make do with less as a one-income home.

Over the years, these costs have occasionally accelerated and come due all at the same time in my life. At those times, I have felt overwhelmed and defeated. I wanted to quit. Yet, because I had counted the cost, I knew I would keep going. One step at a time, I would go forward, trusting God all the way, because I knew that my house was worth building.

Sometimes, though, I have made the building process more costly than God ever intended it to be. Like other homeschooling mothers who live under the fear of not doing enough, I expected more of myself than God did. Consequently, I set unrealistic goals and higher standards for my children than God required. It shouldn't be surprising, then, that I burned out trying to pay a cost God never required. I burned out not because God was asking more of me than I could do, but because I was asking more of me than I could do. As a wiser woman now, I know that God's goal for me is that I build a good house, not the best one. After all, if I become spiritually exhausted because I try to build more than God expects of me, then I soon won't be building at all.

Along the way, I have met mothers who did not count the cost before choosing to homeschool. And when the difficult times came, they decided it must not have been God's will for them after all. It was too hard. So they gave up, put their children back in school and busied themselves with other pursuits. Fortunately I have also met, and regularly fellowship with, many more mothers who have counted the cost. They know there is a price to pay, but they also know there is a reward to enjoy. They are the ones who keep going, even when it is hard, and who keep me going.

When Clay and I built those two houses, the work was tedious, messy, time-consuming and frustrating. We experienced setbacks, our original plans changed, but we kept building. Eventually we enjoyed and benefited from our efforts. It was worth building. And even though the cost is high, your family is worth building.

ᴥ

As I grow older, God opens my eyes a little more each day to see the preciousness and fragility of my children's lives. And each day, I lean a little harder on the Lord. Each day, my confidence and faith for building my own home rests a little less on my abilities and strengths as a mother, and more and more on his character and grace.

One thing I am more confident about than ever, though, is God's faithfulness to godly parents. If I am ordering my life according to the Creator's design for family, I don't have to wonder if my house will stand or fall—it *will* stand. And I can rest assured that the same gracious God who entrusted four precious, fragile lives into *my* hands, will be faithful to keep those children in *his* hands. He will build a home through me, and a testimony through my children, that will stand here on this earth, and throughout eternity.

I'm counting on that, because there is a young girl sitting across from me on my bed who is looking to me for wisdom. I believe the best that I can give her is to prepare her to be a home builder, too. I pray that she will find the same fulfillment I have found in building my house for God.

❦

Thoughts On the Living Word

When the writers of the Old Testament spoke of a "house," the word they used could refer either to a physical structure, or to the people who lived within it. When the writer of Proverbs 24:3 says "the wise woman builds her house," he doesn't mean that she was hauling timbers, stacking mud bricks, and spreading on mortar. He is saying that the wise woman builds her family. She uses timbers of wisdom; she uses bricks of understanding; and she uses the mortar of knowledge. She is careful to use the best building materials that will keep her family standing strong generation after generation. No matter what physical house they may be living in, it is the spiritual house that the wise woman labors hard to build.

Proverbs 24:2,4

The writer of this proverb also pictures a "house" as much more than just a physical structure. What does it mean to build your house with "wisdom"? What is an "established" house? How does "understanding" help bring that about? What kinds of "treasures" fill the house because of "knowledge"? What kinds of treasures fill your house?

Psalm 127

The psalmist reflects on the work of God in building cities and families. What does it mean for the Lord to build a house? What would make your labor vain? Why are children a "reward" from the Lord? How are your children like "arrows" in your hands? What contemporary metaphor could you use instead? How has God "blessed" your home and family?

Matthew 7:24-27

Jesus concludes his Sermon on the Mount with a parable that illustrates the importance of building your home on the right foundation. According to Jesus, how can you build your house to stand, even through the hard storms of life? What does "rock" look like in your home? In what ways are you tempted to build on sand?

Luke 14:28-30

Jesus instructs his followers concerning what it will take to be his disciple. Like the man building a "tower," what will it cost you to build your house? What changes should you make in your life in order to be sure you finish what you have begun to build? Do you know what you are trying to build? Describe it.

My Thoughts

Thoughts On Living the Word

There's something about writing down what I want to accomplish in my children's lives that makes me accountable to what God is saying to me. About once a year, I find time to think about where I want my children to be in 3-5 years, and to plan what I should do to help that happen. ❧ I'll think through areas that help me focus my life as mother—qualities I can build into my children's lives; ways I need to grow and mature; changes I need to make in my life; and so on. As I record my thoughts in my journal, a plan for what I need to do now begins to take shape. ❧ With my "plan" in mind, I'll make a date with each child to go to a special place of their choosing for a time with "just Mom." I will take the time to affirm the ways I see them growing and let them know they are special to me and to God. I'll ask them to share with me their dreams and desires. Then I'll share with them some of my hopes and desires for their lives. It has always been a very special time.

My Life

Personal application: Identify one or two specific character qualities in your life that you need to work on. Determine what the "cost" will be to build that character into your life. Take one step this week toward paying that cost.

Family application: Plan a weekend family night. Using whatever building materials you have (wood blocks, Legos, Duplos, Lincoln Logs), build two houses—one on a pile of popcorn, and one on the solid floor. Eat the popcorn and discuss together Matthew 7:24-27.

"Our deeds, our priorities, our values will come home to rest in our front yards through the lives of our children...Beating within the heart of every decent parent is a desire to set our children on the right course."

Rolf Zettersten
Train Up A Child

Chapter Five

Planning to Live

*Teach us to number our days aright, that we
may gain a heart of wisdom.*

Ⓐs I surveyed the piles of unopened mail, the multiple loads of dirty laundry, the bulging suitcases yet to be unpacked, and the impatiently blinking red light on the answering machine signaling a seemingly infinite number of calls awaiting my attention, I made a quiet vow. I was going to whip our lives into shape or know the reason why!

We had been home only 30 minutes after a fun but exhausting two thousand mile trip, yet it was long enough to realize that I could easily be overwhelmed by the tasks before me. I was determined not to let that happen. This had been the first summer we had taken off from homeschooling in several years, and I knew that we all desperately needed to return to the routines of a disciplined life to keep everything in balance.

Early the next day, I resolutely pulled out my planning sheets and began to write down goals for each of my children. I needed to get focused on homeschooling. First, I determined our Bible reading and discussion, and planned which verses we would memorize. Next, I tackled the educational goals—math, handwriting, language arts, books to read aloud, history, and nature studies. Finally, I planned in the extras—special units, field trips, lessons, and group activities. I studied my completed planning sheets, feeling more confident that our family life would soon begin to fall into place. That confidence would be short-lived.

While I was still fresh from my encouraging time of planning, I received a discouraging call from my mother. My sweet Uncle Frank had died. He had not been well, but his death took us all by surprise. I grieved for the passing of the wonderful man who had always been a part of my family life growing up, but I also found myself grieving for the death of the plans I had made for my own family. I knew this would mean more time away from home and additional days or weeks before I could get back to the plans I had laid out. I quickly packed and traveled to Oklahoma to honor my quiet, easy-going, sweet-hearted Uncle Frank.

The church was full for the funeral service. As I sat in the pew studying the people who had come to remember Frank, I was struck by the variety of people who seemed to be deeply affected by this quiet and gentle man's death. His family, of course, felt the loss the greatest—his sweet wife (my Aunt Mary), his children and grandchildren, and other family close to him. But I also noticed a great number of men his age who were visibly saddened. And I noticed numerous teenaged young men and women who had come, and who seemed especially sad.

I didn't know very many of the people who were there, but I knew why they were there. Their lives had been touched by a man known for his kind words, generous spirit and servant's heart. He was always helping someone else, doing for others, lending a hand. For years he attended all the sports activities of his children and grandchildren, driving the family station wagon loaded with their young friends to and from the games. He was the kind of man who was a friend to anyone he met.

The eulogies revealed what everyone seemed to already know and feel about Uncle Frank. But I caught myself thinking about what they weren't saying. No one praised his abilities in math, or his proficiency in language arts, or his knowledge of historical facts. Those things, I thought to myself, contributed to what he would become and do with his life, but at the end of his life they mattered little. Neither did anyone care at that point what he could've done but didn't, or what position in life he did or didn't attain, or how much money and how many things he had acquired. What mattered most is that he had taken the time to invest in the most important things in life—the lives of people.

As I drove back home to Texas, God impressed on my heart that I needed to reconsider my plans. The funeral had refocused my thoughts, and now I needed to refocus my plans. Some day my children will die, and their own lives will be eulogized. I want to be sure that their lives will be measured by the right standard. If they are known only for what they have learned, or achieved, or accumulated, then I will have missed the mark. I want them to be known and remembered for the size of their hearts, and for the number of lives they have touched for eternity!

When I got home, I went back to my planning sheets and started again. Sure, I still needed to do the things I had planned, but this time I started with a different focus. Rather than the focus of achieving educational goals, I started with a focus on building into my children's lives what will count for eternity. That wasn't a particularly new thought to me, but Uncle Frank's funeral had reminded me that I need to stick to my priority of training my children with their eternity in view, not just their years on this earth! That focus must never change.

I know I can't neglect the basic educational foundations my children will need for a full and meaningful life—reading and understanding the written word, thinking clearly and wisely, communicating ably in speech and in writing, and being competent in math. But I am determined not to neglect the basic spiritual truth that will undergird and give meaning to that education—"Seek first the kingdom of God and his righteousness." A well-educated person will be useful to God only if he is focused on God's purposes.

And so, with my heart focused again where it should have been to begin with, I began planning what I could do this year to prepare my children to serve the Lord. It helped me to look at my goals from three perspectives: What do I want my children to *know*? What do I want my children to *be*? What do I want my children to *do*?

What I want my children to know

Never before in the history of our young nation has the battle for the mind been waged so fiercely. The biblical values and morals that once were considered commonplace in America now are called out-of-place by an increasingly secular society that has shoved God and the Bible aside in favor of man-made truths. As a mother, there is a deep sorrow in my soul that my children will grow up in a culture that is not at all like the one I grew up in. But there is also a deep conviction that I must prepare them to live in that culture where their beliefs will be constantly challenged and ridiculed, and might even become the cause of personal persecution. I know that I must prepare their minds with biblical truth and a Christian worldview if they are to keep the faith in a hostile culture.

What they become as adults and what they do with their lives will depend in large measure on what they know about God. If I want their lights to shine brightly in the darkness that pervades this world as they grow up, then I must light strong fires of truth in their minds now. A weak flame will easily be blown out by the winds of false teaching and deception; a strong flame will only become brighter and stronger. If I do nothing else in my children's lives, I must be sure that the flame of God's truth is burning strongly and brightly before I release them to their world.

I cannot begin to summarize here all the deep and lifechanging truths that I want my children to know, the truths that have sustained the church for 2000 years, and the truths that have guided my own Christian life for over 25 years. God's word is simply too rich and too deep to reduce those truths to a few words. Yet I know it all begins with an exalted view of our

God, the One who created us, sustains us, and redeems us.

I want to drive deep into my children's developing minds a picture of God's greatness, holiness, justice and righteousness. I want them to fear and respect the all-powerful, transcendent God of all creation. Yet in all his greatness and majesty, he is also a personal God, tenderly leading and caring for those who are his. I want my children to know that he is real, that he is intimately involved in their lives, and that he is sovereign and in control of all the circumstances and events of their lives, good or bad. I want them to know Jesus, God become man, as their personal Savior and Lord, bridging the great eternal chasm between holy God and sinful man. I want them to know the faithfulness and lovingkindness of our God, that nothing can separate them from him once they are adopted into his eternal family, and that they can have confidence in this life because they know they are secure in the hands of their Creator and Savior. I want them to know all this and so much more.

Beyond the knowledge of these life-shaping truths, I want them to understand that God has stamped their souls with his image, and as his image-bearers they can be a picture of God for the lost world in which they will live and minister as God's people. The knowledge of God that they take into adulthood is not meant to stop with them, but they are to be a channel of that truth to others, shining the light of his truth in the darkness of their generation.

Jeremiah, God's messenger of judgment to Judah, is a good example of living as a channel of God's truth in a world of darkness. For years, he had warned the people of Judah that God would judge them if they did not repent and turn back to him, just as he had the ten tribes of Israel in the north. Though he spoke the truth, he was rejected, castigated, and scorned by his people, those who once followed God but now looked for truth from man-made gods (sound familiar?).

After the destruction of Jerusalem and the exile of the Jews to Babylon, Jeremiah laments all that has happened to him, his land, and his people. His response, recorded in the book of Lamentations, reveals a man whose mind was anchored by a deep and profound understanding of God. His light was not extinguished by the terrible events he had witnessed, nor was his view of God diminished. Despite everything, he was still able to say, "This I call to mind, therefore I have hope. The Lord's lovingkindnesses indeed never cease, for his compassions never fail. They are new every morning; Great is Your faithfulness." (Lam. 3:21-23, NASB) What he knew to be true about God, enabled him to trust God to be true to his character.

This year, I want my children to get to know the God that Jeremiah trusted, the same God that we trust today. Through study, discussion, and memorization, I want to drive those truths deep into their minds. Perhaps, some day, they will need to call them to mind, so they can have hope. If they do, I know that my God will be faithful.

What I want my children to be

My children will be known not just for what they know, but for what kind of people they become. Character speaks louder than words! As they grow in their knowledge of who God is and what he expects of them in this life, they will begin to face the personal challenge of becoming what God wants them to be. My goal is to guide them in the development of godly character. Though they will have to decide within themselves whether or not they will conform their lives to God's character, it is my role to help them stay on the path of life that God has set before us as a family until they are ready to walk it by themselves.

Knowing from experience that even seemingly good playmates can become a bad influence on my children, I was especially cautious when our whole family became involved with a large ministry project over several months. Due to the nature of the ministry, we weren't always able to stay together as a family. The younger children were generally supervised by an adult, but the kids all had a lot of freedom to run around the area and play together. It was not an ideal situation, but we trusted our children. We felt better when my boys met another boy whose parents had a good reputation as mature Christians. He impressed my boys, too, because he seemed very generous, and he always had a fascinating story to tell about what he had done or where he had been.

Over a period of time, though, we noticed that our children avoided playing with this naturally outgoing and outspoken boy. It turned out that what he said could not be trusted. They told us how he would take soft drinks without paying for them, and how he tried to impress other children with the profane words that he knew. It became very evident that this child knew all of the right things to say in front of adults, but his actions with my children revealed his real character. Fortunately, my boys were not attracted to this kind of friendship and found other children to pal around with.

This little boy, because of his parents, will probably turn out fine. Others like him, though, may not. They will learn too soon to enjoy playing in the weeds along the path of life. They are just a few steps away from exploring the dark shadows in the forests of sin that lie beyond the path. That realization is a picture for me of what I must be doing in my children's lives. I am a guide, a teacher, and a protector to them as they are beginning their own journey along the path of life. I am responsible for helping them develop the godly character and habits that will keep them on God's path of righteousness and life. Without that training, they might be easily tempted to wander off the path and suffer the character-killing effects of sin. Even though they might know the wonderful truths of God and even impress others with their knowledge, that knowledge will be empty and vain unless it is accompanied by a growing godly character.

God has not given precise instructions in the Bible, so there is no easy formula for how to develop character in children. I've found, though, that the picture of the "path of life" from Proverbs gives me a way to visualize my role in the process of character training. As a "guide," I am leading the way, modeling what it means to live a godly life, and providing directions whenever they are needed. As a "teacher," I am always learning and sharing what I have learned about living the godly life. As a "protector," I am constantly watching and guarding my children's steps to be sure they stay on the path, confronting sins and sinful attitudes that might lead them astray.

I cannot make my children mature all at once, but I can help them grow in godliness one quality at a time. This year, in addition to new areas of character I want to instill in my children, I am also concerned about some weak areas in their lives that I need to work on. I have seen laziness and anger in one child, lack of initiative and follow through in another, and self-centeredness and insensitivity in another. Step by step, I want to lead them a little further along the path of life to become strong in godly character.

What I want my children to do

Finally, I know that it is not enough to raise children into adults who only know God's word and walk in God's ways. Knowing and being are critical to my child's maturity, but to be fully trained, they must also *do God's work*. That is what it means to have integrity as a Christian—to be fully integrated with God's purposes. God's truth may fill their minds, and his Spirit may be at work in their hearts, but the process is incomplete until the passion of Jesus for the lost and hurting, and for the needs of the world, moves their hands to reach out to the people he died for.

The disciples of Jesus certainly had many strong memories of the Lord powerfully teaching God's truth, and there is no doubt that they were drawn to his perfect, sinless character. But surely the most profound impact upon the disciples came as they watched Jesus minister! He fed five thousand with food enough for only five, he confronted and cast out demons, he calmed storms, and raised the dead. He reached out to the hurting and gave them hope, he healed the sick and the afflicted, and he touched the untouchables and gave them love. His touch changed lives. He washed the disciples' feet as a common servant would, and he cooked them a meal and ministered to them, even after they had all deserted him at his time of greatest need. And they saw him die on the cross for their sins, an act of ultimate service, and be raised again from the dead. All of these acts of service were burned into the disciples' minds. And when the Holy Spirit gave birth to the church, it was this ministry to others that would set it apart as somthing different.

There is no doubt in my mind that personal ministry is the missing measure of Christian maturity in the evangelical church today. Truth and character alone do not fully define a mature Christian. God has convicted me of this personally, but I also believe that the Christian homeschooling movement has unintentionally adopted a ministry-less measure of maturity for our children. It is so easy to be busy all the time, to focus on academics, to be intent on character training, and yet neglect to give our children specific ways to work out in the lives of people what God is working into their minds and hearts.

My children need to have a ministry. However small or trivial it may seem, they need me to help them develop the passion for and the habit of serving other people in the Lord's name. In fact, even though it is now the "day of small things," I want them to dream of big things they can do to reach out, minister, and serve. I want them to grow up not just believing, but seeing that God will use even the smallest servant to accomplish great things for his kingdom.

However, if I want my children to have a heart for the lost, they must see me reaching out to the lost with a passion for their souls. If I want them to have a heart to serve others, they must see me serving others joyfully and without complaint. If I want them to have a heart for missions, they must see me praying for and supporting missionaries. If I want them to honor and serve other adults, they must see me honor and serve their needs, the needs of their friends, and of all who enter our home. Even as the disciples saw Jesus model servanthood before their eyes day after day, so my children will notice and respond to my example if they see me serving them and others in our home day after day with a thankful and joyful heart.

Practically, this part of my life requires careful and strategic planning, or else it will be swept aside in the rush of a busy life. It is my responsibility to create opportunities for my children to minister to others—to generously share their money, food, or toys; to give up their bedrooms for traveling missionaries; to volunteer for childcare during the church meetings; to serve meals at a homeless shelter; to teach a smaller children's Sunday school class; to visit a nursing home.

I also want to be sure I am helping each of my children to develop a heart for serving others spontaneously—to give up their seat to an adult; to carry a heavy package for an elderly person; to clean up the kitchen or the yard; to play with a toddler. In our home, our children have served meals for unexpected visitors, cared for the children of mothers who needed counseling, cleaned, cooked, and hosted Christian gatherings in our home. Even now, they have taken turns caring for Joy while I write this book. These are not just assigned duties and responsibilities, but acts of unselfish service that are training their hearts to look beyond their own needs, and to consider the needs of others first (Phil. 2:3-4).

I have often noticed that giving our children opportunities to serve builds up their sense of self-importance. Our support group used to go to the retirement home to help the residents celebrate birthdays once a month. It was so sweet to see my boys very gently pushing the wheel chairs down the hall to the birthday party, patting the old people on the knee, serving them cake and talking loudly into their ears. It was as though giving them something important to do made them act as though they were important!

We all remember reading aloud as a family a biography about Brother Andrew, a missionary to Eastern Europe and Russia after the war when they were behind the Iron Curtain. The story of his life excited the children's imaginations as they heard how God did miracles in and through the life of an ordinary man. But when we actually traveled to Russia in real life, and saw first-hand how people in those countries lived, then my children became excited about how God might use *them*. We met with missionaries in their small, cramped apartments and heard stories about their ministries. We performed in *The Promise* in the Kremlin Palace Theatre before thousands of Russians each night and saw that the message of Christ made them cry and beg for more. We saw the ruined lives of the drunken and partying people in our hotel who needed the gospel so badly. My children saw needs that God might someday use them to meet.

᠈ᴥ

Paul admonished believers to "be careful how you walk, not as unwise men but as wise, making the most of your time, because the days are evil" (Eph. 5:17-18, NASB). Another more literal translation says we are to "redeem the time." The Greek word Paul uses is the same term used to describe the action of someone who would pay the price to free a person from slavery. Paul suggests that the brief time we are given on this earth can be redeemed, too. In other words, we should understand that our time is enslaved to the world, but we can buy it back and set it free to be useful to God. In the face of an "evil" world, we are called by God to be "careful" and to be "wise" in the use of our time. Paul's admonition closely echoes Moses' words: "So teach us to number our days, that we may present to You a heart of wisdom" (Ps. 90:12, NASB).

But parents receive a double dose of this principle. In addition to ourselves, we are also called to do the same for our children, who are under our care and guidance—to make the most of their time, and to number their days. No matter how it may appear to you when you observe the lives of your children when they are young, they are a reflection of your own commitments and priorities. If it seems like they waste their time or squander their days, then it is your responsibility to make the most of their time and to number their days for them. God has given you, their parent, the opportunity to guide your children according to what you see is God's will for their lives—what they should know, be, and do.

Books and curriculum are important, but only as they serve to prepare your children for God's purposes for their lives. Don't let academics become the focus of your planning when you think about your children's lives. Be sure your focus is on eternal issues, on the areas that prepare their heads, hearts, and hands to be useful to God—knowing God's truth, becoming godly people, and doing God's work of ministry and service. These are the priorities that will give them an excitement for using their academic training, and their gifts and abilities, for God's purposes.

Then, regardless how they do on Achievement Tests or on the S.A.T., you can know that your children will score high on God's achievement test of life. That's the one that will really count, because it will count for eternity.

❧

Thoughts On the Living Word

Godly values have always been in conflict with worldly values, but perhaps the lines have never been drawn so clearly and so often as in our present culture. Godly values are challenged and ridiculed at every turn by the media and the great institutions of our day, while worldly values are presented as normal and desirable. If we don't know our priorities as Christians in this life, it is easy to be worn down by the sheer overload of worldly propaganda. Our children are even more vulnerable to the onslaught of worldliness, and in need of our protection and confident leadership. But Scripture is full of wisdom for making the right choices, and for living a life on godly principles. We just have to believe it, and do it.

Philippians 3:1-11

The Apostle Paul defended his ministry by drawing the lines between what he was and could have been, and what he is and desires to be. What would Paul's "resume" sound like today? What things must you "consider loss for the sake of Christ"? How valuable is it to you to "gain Christ"? Is your source of confidence the same as Paul's?

Ephesians 5:8-17

Paul exhorts the readers of his letter to be careful how they live now that they are believers. What does it mean to be "children of light"? Have you found out what "pleases the Lord"? How are you being "careful" in your life as a Christian mother? Are you "making the most of every opportunity" in your life? How are you doing the same in your children's lives?

John 13:1-17

At the Last Supper with his disciples, Jesus demonstrates his greatest desire for them. How would you feel if Jesus, the Creator of all things, washed your feet as a lowly servant would? Why did Jesus consider the quality of servanthood so important? How do you model this kind of servanthood to your children?

Psalm 90

Moses prays for compassion on sinful Israel, and he expresses a realistic understanding of our frailty and the shortness of our lives. Does your life seem long or short when you read this psalm? What is the point of learning to "number our days" if they are so few and fleeting? What is Moses' desire for Israel? What is your desire for your family?

My Thoughts

Thoughts On Living the Word

One of the easiest ways I have found to be sure I am focusing on God's priorities with my children is to talk about God with them, and to teach them while I talk. Even within a normal conversation during the day, I can talk about an attribute of God, define it, discuss it, and quote a scripture about it. ❧ Clay and I try to get away together throughout the year to review our goals and plans, and to pray together about them. Every family has its own way of planning, but I always try to find the easiest and quickest method of getting my thoughts down on paper. It might be as easy as listing out together what we want our children to know, to be, and to do over the coming months. ❧ Whenever we plan ministry projects for our family, we try to let the children be as involved as possible. We've had several "brainstorming" sessions to consider different kinds of ministries. When God puts something on all our hearts, we'll plan it together. The children always have ideas and insights to offer.

My Life

Personal application: Spend some time this week with Ephesians 5:8-17. List anything you do with your children that "pleases the Lord." Then, list some ways you need to be "careful." Finally, identify some specific opportunties you can "make the most of," and how you will.

Family application: Make a Know-Be-Do-Be-Do poster for each child. Choose a verse together that you want each child to "know." Then identify two character qualities you want them to develop ("be"), and have them come up with two ministry things they will "do."

"As the hand is made for holding and the eye for seeing, You have fashioned me for joy. Share with me the vision that shall find it everywhere; in the wild violet's beauty; in the lark's melody; in the face of a steadfast man; in a child's smile; in a mother's love; in the purity of Jesus."

Gaelic prayer
in Lord Bless My Child

Chapter Six

Surprised by Joy

*I have no greater joy than to hear that my
children are walking in the truth.*

The end of summer was near and the promise of autumn drew us irresistibly out of the house into a delightful afternoon. The air was unusually cool, the sun was shining in full force, and the skies were a stunning blue. It was a perfect day to explore the hike-and-bike trails in the sprawling nature center behind our house that seemed like an extension of our backyard. The girls were content to follow at a slower pace, while Clay and the boys donned biking helmets, jumped on their trail bikes, and took off in the lead for our grand adventure.

Sarah decided she would walk and talk with me as I pushed baby Joy in her stroller. As we leisurely strolled along the trail on the top of the river levy, we talked about everyday life, casually sharing ideas, feelings, and plans about our week. It seemed such a luxury to have this relaxed time outdoors. Joy demanded that we stop every few minutes while she picked up another leaf to add to the growing collection she was clutching in her chubby little hands. She seemed happy just to shout out her new word to anyone who would listen, "Lee! Lee!" Then, as if to say, "I realize you don't know what I am saying," she would hold up her leaf bouquet to be sure we caught her meaning.

The boys, meanwhile, biked energetically up and down the trails, always huffing and puffing their way back to us to tell about the people they had seen, the dogs they had met, or some other interesting observation from a boy's point-of-view. As they rode away at high speed, pumping the pedals as hard as they could, there would always be some trick jump attempted, or a tall hill scaled, or a kid-sized wheelie, followed by a, "Hey, Mom, did you see that!" Dad, all the while, was taking his time and enjoying the trail at a more "mature" pace. Sarah and I waved our admiration to our three talented men, smiling with feminine wonder at the budding masculinity on display before us. Sarah then turned to me with a look of contentedness and shared, "I feel so good when we are all together and close. I'll bet it must be lonely to be in school and not be able to be together all the time."

I knew just what she meant. I love it when we are all together as a family, feeling like we are an integral part of each other's lives. It feels so natural and normal, the way it should be. I believe God meant us to feel fulfilled in family because it satisfies our need for a place to belong, a place where you know you fit in. In our family, there is always someone around to admire a new car that Joel has designed, or to enjoy a new piano arrange-ment that Sarah has mastered, or to be impressed at the new Civil War outfit that Nathan has put together, or just to clap for Joy when she takes her medicine without spitting it out on Mom or Dad. Everything is a group activity in our home.

These kinds of joyful moments catch me by surprise. I'm not looking for them, or expecting them, but all of a sudden my eyes are opened and I discover another of the joys that God meant for me to know. It was there all along, but I had missed it. The joys get lost in the blur of too many activi-ties, and dimmed by a nearsightedness that sees only the housework that must be done, the educational goals that must be achieved, and the needs that must be met. It shouldn't be a surprise to me that there would be all kinds of joys just waiting to blossom out of the family and home-centered lifestyle of homeschooling. If that is how God meant us to live, then he wants to bless us through it. Nevertheless, I find myself delightfully surprised by the joy of the life God has given me.

ॐ

In the autumn of his life, after living as a confirmed bachelor, C.S. Lewis was surprised by an unexpected romance. This proper professor of English Literature had never fancied himself a romantic, but Joy Gresham, an American woman, blew the dust off his heart that had gathered there during his years of academic isolation amid the books of Oxford. What started as a very formal relationship, culminated in marriage. He was delightfully surprised by the joy he discovered in his relationship with her. Even when cancer invaded her body, and death robbed him of Joy, Lewis was yet able to give testimony to a joy and fulfillment from God in their relationship that he had never before known, or even known about.

I came to homeschooling much as C.S. Lewis probably came to his relationship with Joy Gresham. I looked at it initially as a formal procedure, the means to an end. I was convinced and convicted that homeschooling was the best way for me to disciple my children. I also believed it was the best choice for educating them, and for shaping their minds with the truths and ideas that were important to Clay and me. But I wasn't really thinking about whether or not it would be enjoyable, only that it was the right thing to do.

Now, though, I am almost daily, it seems, surprised by some new joy that I had not expected to find in this homeschooling lifestyle. I feel I can almost see the Lord smiling with delight whenever I discover one of his new blessings that I had never anticipated, just as I myself do when I see one of my children find a surprise I have put out for them to enjoy. It is these joyous surprises that keep me going, so I wanted to share some of them with you. Maybe you haven't discovered some of them yet. I know I haven't discovered all of them yet, but I'm looking for them now.

Surprised by the joy of opening minds

It is so easy to take learning for granted. When I was growing up, there was very little wonder or excitement in it, just the duty of studying and making good grades. Consequently, the best part of school was not the learning part, but the playing part. I can imagine now, though, how hard it would be for any one teacher to truly express the excitement and wonder of learning to 20-30 young children passing through her classroom every nine months. That would require an enormous emotional reserve, or a very special gift for teaching.

When I first came to homeschooling, I brought along some wrong thinking. I simply assumed and expected that educating my children was going to be a lot of work, both for me and my children. I suppose that such a pessimistic view was partly the legacy of my own classroom experiences. And even though I had earned a teaching certificate in college, and done some student teaching, I lacked the confidence that I could teach my children to read. I just knew I couldn't succeed without professional help!

I struggled with these areas briefly until I stumbled upon a truth that seems obvious now, but was a new revelation at the time—I didn't have to teach my children how to learn. God had already prepared them to learn, and I just needed to give them room. I am simply a facilitator, releasing skills and abilities already there in my children. That was an unanticipated surprise.

I was so wonderfully surprised when I had the privilege of watching my children's reading skills blossom and grow with just direction and encouragement. It seemed like a miracle to me. All I did was sit with them, day by day, reviewing their letters and sounds, and helping them sound out words. Yet they learned to read! It had much less to do with my skill and knowledge as a teacher, and everything to do with their God-given, inherent abilities. I just sat back in awe and wonder when they suddenly took off and began to read without me. From then on, I was just along for the learning-to-read ride.

As their reading continued to naturally improve, I watched their little minds sharpen before my very eyes. Their insights about life became deeper, their knowledge broader, and their wisdom clearer. To quench their God-given thirst for learning, they drank deeply from our library, and overflowed with good ideas in thought-provoking conversations. It has been such a wonderful experience to read aloud with my children, and for me to learn so many new and interesting things right along with them. And to think it happened all within the walls of my humble home, without a student desk in sight. What a deeply satisfying and surprising joy it has been for me to discover that my children came prepared by God to learn.

Surprised by the joy of softening spirits

Though bemoaned by so many as the "terrible twos," I have found those years to be some of the most exciting in my children's lives. It is the time in their young lives when they first begin to discover and exercise their newfound "will." I'll admit that it sometimes seems more like a "won't" than a "will," but those first signs of emerging personality and conscience are wonderful to watch. It is a profound time of development in their lives. The will that will allow them to respond freely to God is breaking through, and I'm there to watch it and guide it, from its first faltering steps of independence, all the way through to the time when it is yielded to God to do his will in dependence upon him.

I didn't realize how fulfilling it would be to walk with my children day-by-day as their spirits softened to God. What an unexpected joy it has been to talk to our children every day about Jesus, to tell them of his love for us, and our love for him, and to see them begin to love him in their own ways. I have patiently explained God's plan for their lives, wondering if they were paying any attention, then listened in amazement in other conversations as my instruction came back to me with clarity and insight. As I have watched each of them begin to pray to God, I have sent my own prayers of thanks and praise back to the Father for his work in their lives. And, of course, what a joyful experience it has been for Clay and me to gently guide our children to the Savior and see them receive him into their hearts.

It should not have been surprising to me, but it was, that children so young could have such deep thoughts about God and eternity, and disturbing doubts as well. But it has been so rewarding to have my children come to me with their doubts and struggles, to talk about them, to search the scriptures, to give them answers, and to reassure their spirits. What a joy I would miss if I were not there, and my children had no one like me to talk with them about what they had heard or thought. Or worse, if they turned to someone else!

There is nothing quite like the experience of handing down to my children our family's convictions and values about the Christian life. We want them to believe what we believe about the Bible, marriage, sex, family, femininity and masculinity, leadership, service, temptation, sin, gifts, ministry, and so many more areas. It has been a surprising and deeply satisfying joy for me to know that I have had the privilege of shaping and filling my children's hearts. I don't think it occurred to me before we began this homeschooling journey just how jealous I would be for their hearts, and how protective I would be of the ideas and values we give them that would be challenged by others outside our family unit. But how glad I am that I have them to train and to shape.

Surprised by the joy of emerging maturity

There have been times when I wondered whether or not my boys were really becoming any more mature. I would pray, exhort, instruct, and train, but there seemed to be little consistency in their progress. It was frustrating. But Clay reminded me that children, especially the boy-types, all of a sudden will turn a corner and enter a new phase of maturity. So, I patiently waited and, while I wasn't looking at them quite so intently, they changed. Just like that. Around the ages of 8 and 10, they just became something new right before my eyes, and they began to grow in areas where before they had seemed forever stuck in immaturity. It is such a wonderful experience to watch that happen.

Housework has become a kind of litmus test of emerging maturity for my children. I have struggled with it for years, never quite reaching the standards that I brought to marriage from the home I grew up in (which was kept neat and clean by a full-time maid!). Despite my housekeeping handicap, though, I have consistently tried to train into each of my children the work habits and personal responsibility that are required for life. I have been pleasantly surprised, in spite of my own weaknesses, that my children are becoming mature in their ability to help with housework. They straighten a room to make it look nice with relatively little effort, they can place a nice meal on the table for our family, they are actually friendly and gracious when others come to our house, and they can take care of guests all by themselves.

In spite of all our own ups and downs, bad habits, weaknesses, inconsistencies, immaturity and blind spots, our children continue to grow and mature. They aren't perfect, but they're getting better all the time. At this point, that is enough for me! I have to admit, I find myself looking forward to those corners yet to be turned, and wondering how I'll be amazed at their growth on the other side. Yet even while they're still on their way to the corner, I am constantly surprised by the nice, interesting, enjoyable people that my children are becoming.

Surprised by the joy of family traditions

It is a rare Sunday that the Clarkson family can't be found gathered around the table, with cups and saucers at each place, a big pot of tea wrapped up in a tea cozy, and a tasty treat waiting to be enjoyed. Or, for a birthday to arrive without my fresh-ground, whole-wheat, homemade cinnamon rolls gracing the table for the family-only birthday celebration breakfast. Or, for Christmas to come and go without our Christmas Eve Shepherds' Meal of soup, cheese, fruit, and homemade bread. Or, for the Labor Day weekend to pass without Family Day, with photo albums reviewed and new "memorial stones" of God's faithfulness carefully drawn and placed in our Family Day Celebration notebook.

All of these traditions shape our identity as a family, and define for our children what family means. When I'm asked as an adult, "What was your family like when you were growing up?" my first thoughts are always about how we celebrated holidays, or what we did at meals, or what kinds of vacations we took. Now, with my own family, I am becoming more aware of the power of traditions to shape my children's mental picture of family. I see myself as an artist, of sorts, drawing and painting in my children's minds a beautiful picture of family that will remain there for the rest of their lives on this earth.

Of course, it's not just the "big" traditions that go into the painting. The holidays and celebrations may create the strongest lines of the picture I am creating, but it's the "little" traditions that add the color and character to my family canvas. I want the memories of what we do to at the dinner table, what we do in the car, the special words and phrases we use, the way we hug, and the way we take family walks to be bright splashes of color in their recollections of family. I want the music we all love to hear and sing, the books we consider "our books," the special movies we watch every year, the favorite places we go to play and relax, and all the myriad other family habits that define us, to add depth and realism to their mental picture of family. And for the deep flesh tones in their family picture, I want my children to remember my nightly prayer whispers in each of their ears, Dad's "fuzzy kisses" with his tickly beard, and all the little daily habits and rituals that bind us together as a family.

It has been such a joy in discovering my new role as a painter of memories. My paints and brushes are all the things I do to build traditions into our home and family life, and my canvas is the minds of my children. That has given me such a renewed joy for refining and strengthening our family traditions. I just love being a family artist!

Surprised by the joy of homemade humor

There is more real humor in an average day of homeschooling a family of four than you can find in a week of television sitcoms. So much of what the world calls "humorous" is either empty, puerile, tasteless, offensive, or lame. It is mostly "cheap" humor that gets a laugh at someone else's expense, or "taboo" humor that tries to make light of what should be kept in the dark. Without the fake humor of the world shaping our children's funny bones, though, it has been such a delight to find the real humor that God has fashioned in our spirits. I see it every day at home, and it has been such a wonderful surprise to rediscover the kind of real-life, homemade humor that God meant us to enjoy.

I laugh just thinking about some of the more recent real-life sitcoms in our family that didn't need a TV. Like the family night when we were studying a scripture about the the contrast between Jesus, who is light, and Satan who represents the darkness in this world. Nathan took the punch line, "Oh, I know what that means—Jesus is the salt, and Satan is the pepper!" Or when, in a rush to get a glass of lemonade for a friend who was visiting in our home, we unknowingly served her a tall, cool glass of *canola oil*! It was sort of yellow, and in the same kind of container, and it brought quite a response from our guest, and a howl of laughter to the room. Or, watching my boys feign torture and pretending to almost pass out when baby joy hugged them and handed them her odorous and very full diaper (what wimps!). This kind of humor needs no trend-concious script writers to create a gag—it's just the normal part of our lives.

My home life is not always filled with humor, but when it is I love the joy of knowing that it is pure and unadulterated (literally) humor. The surprise has been to discover the joy of homemade humor that bubbles up naturally from hearts that belong to the Lord. After all, shouldn't we have the most reason to laugh and enjoy life?

Surprised by the joy of undistracted creativity

The typical classroom is structured to reinforce conformity—give the right answers, do things the right way, speak at the right time, learn by the right methods. It's no surprise to find, then, that the creative flame that burned brightly when most children started school has been all but extinguished by the time they reach the third grade. In stark contrast, the home should be a place to reinforce creativity. The Creator God has left his mark in my children's spirits. I believe my home should be a place where their creativity will burn brightly through all their childhood, fanned into flame by the freedom to learn, discover, and inquire unhindered by institutional barriers and expectations, stoked by the richness and diversity of resources, and fed by an atmosphere of love and acceptance.

I am constantly surprised and amazed by the creativity my children exhibit simply because they have the freedom and resources to exercise their creative powers. I certainly haven't taught my children how to be creative—I've simply created the opportunity and watched with joy as their creative juices flowed. I love to see how they try to create impressive papers on the computer, or tell a story through a series of drawings, or recreate historical vistas with Lego blocks, or come up with solutions for problems, or re-enact historical events with creative costuming, or numerous other creative exercises.

When I first began homeschooling, it had not yet occurred to me that cultivating creativity would be such an important part of my role. Now, I am surprised at how critically important it is to strengthen that creative drive and spirit. But even beyond that, seeing my children's creativity blossom and grow has become one of the areas of homeschooling that I most enjoy. It has definitely been a joyful surprise.

There have been so many other unexpected joys in homeschooling, like the ones above, which have surprised and delighted my spirit. I truly believe that if most people really realized just how personally rewarding and fulfilling the homeschooling lifestyle is, they would want to give it a try. The problem is, you don't really realize it until you've done it for awhile, so few in our culture are willing to head in that direction.

In fact, just the opposite seems to be the norm. We live in a culture in which most families are directionless, adrift on the sea of life. There is no wind of meaning to fill their sails, no currents of purpose to propel them toward a destination. Everyone seems to be alone and isolated in their own boats, rarely connecting with others drifting around them. Most are simply dead in the water.

In our home, in contrast, we are at full sail and riding the strongest currents because we know our destination. We are living by the design of the Creator, and enjoying all the wonderful benefits of family life that he meant us to enjoy. We are never dead in the water, but always alive and brimming with life, always searching the horizon for what we're going to find next on our exciting journey with God. Every day, we are surprised by a new joy discovered on our journey.

Paul did not mince any words on this issue. He commands us in Romans 12:2 not to be conformed to this world, but rather to be trans-formed by the renewing of our minds in Christ. When we do that, he says, we will prove what the will of God is, and that it is good, acceptable and perfect. The world has a very different view of a mother than God's revealed will for mothers. Since the world does not do God's will, its view can be described only as less-than-good, unacceptable, and imperfect. In God's good, acceptable, and perfect design, the mother is at home, nurtur-ing and loving her children, contributing to the spiritual, character, and intellectual training of her children. God's blessings—his joyful surprises—are the natural result of choosing God's will.

Having been on the blessing side of the equation for many years now, I can attest to the truth that there is a great joy in doing God's will. Better yet, it is not a one-time, all-at-once joy, but a continuous, always-more-to-come joy that brings new and delightful surprises every day of this wonderful life God has given me at home.

When I think of little Joy holding up those leaves for me to see, as though she had found something that I had surely never seen before, I think of my relationship with the Lord. How pleasing it must be for him, as we walk together along the path of this life, when I pick up one of the leaves of my life and hold it up to him with joy and excitement. How good it must make him feel to see me holding those living leaves like special treasures. In the same way that my heart was delighted with my little Joy's discoveries, I feel sure that God's heart is similarly delighted by my joy in finding the many blessings he has let fall into my life.

Of course, Joy herself is one of those blessings. There was no greater surprise in my life than when, in my forties, I was "surprised by Joy." The baby toys and clothes had been sold just the week before when I discovered I was pregnant with my fourth child. Though we didn't realize it at the time, Joy's name would be almost prophetic. It is she who has brought such joy to our lives at a time when we were least expecting it. Having her fall into our lives opened my eyes anew to the wonderful blessings of God in my life, to all the other joyful surprises that I sometimes don't look for. How thankful I am, as I hold her up to God with a smile, that he allowed me to be surprised by Joy, because she has taught me to be surprised by joy every day.

❧

Thoughts On the Living Word

Eternal life does not start after we die. It is a quality of life we enjoy from the moment of rebirth. Though we cannot escape suffering in this temporal life, God's desire for us is to fully enjoy the eternal life he has given us, not just at some point in the distant future, but from the moment our spirit is regenerated with new life by the Holy Spirit. He brings a freshness, vitality, and purpose to life that is impossible to experience when you are separated from the true Giver of Life. As a "new creation," you begin to see life in an entirely new way—every day is a discovery, every problem an opportunity for faith, every relationship an adventure. Without the Holy Spirit to correct our spiritual eyesight, we will be spiritually nearsighted, seeing only this life. With him, we see the life to come. That makes all the difference.

John 15:1-17

Jesus teaches his disciples that real life comes only from being attached to him, the vine. Is your life "fruitful" or fruitless? How are you attached to the "vine"? How important is "love" in your life? How do you and your family "remain" (or, "abide") in Christ's love? How does that make your life joyful?

John 7:37-39

Jesus stood up in the hearing of the people gathered for the feast in Jerusalem to invite them to believe on him. What would you think if you were in the crowd and heard the words of Jesus? How would his "streams of living water" change your life? How are you offering that living water to your children?

Philippians 1:3-11

Paul writes to his faithful Philippian friends. How confident are you of God completing the "good work" that he has begun in you? Why is Paul's affection so deep for the Philippian church? What kind of life does he pray that they will have? What kind of life do you pray that you will have?

Romans 12:1,2

Paul encourages his readers to act upon the truths he has laid out in the previous eleven chapters. How can you and your family offer yourselves as "living sacrifices" to God? What kind of life does Paul imply comes from being "transformed"? What does it mean to have your mind "renewed"?

My Thoughts

Thoughts On Living the Word

One exercise I have used to give myself a spiritual lift is to write in my journal, or on a piece of notepaper, all of the memories of my children that bring me the most joy. Or, I will identify as many things about homeschooling as I can that have been the greatest benefit or blessing to me and our family. ❧ I'm always on the lookout for good greeting cards that I can give to Clay and the children. Occasionally, even though there is no birthday or holiday in sight, I'll pick a meaningful card and write a note on it to express specific ways that one of them has brought joy and happiness into my life. Sometimes, rather than leaving it somewhere for them to find, I'll put a stamp on it and mail it. ❧ If I want my children to sense the same joy and blessing that I do out of life, then I need to make life in my home enjoyable for them. I find, though, that I have to make a willful decision to do that with so many "duties" that beckon. I try to make it a habit to listen to their desires, to play games with them, to read books to them, and so on.

My Life

Personal application: Your children are a result of God's living water flowing through your life. Take some time to slowly and reflectively look at your family photos or photo album to remind yourself of how God has been working in your family through you.

Family application: Make a spiritual fruit tree (use your creativity). Jesus is the center vine, each branch a family member. During the week, "fruit" is hung upon the tree when a family member does something that brings joy. Goal: to have others fill up your branch.

Fall ~ Season *of* Resolve

Fall

Thoughts on Resolve
Ten Years Later

Thursday afternoon marked the end of the hustle and bustle of getting Sarah and Joel off to begin their eight-week journey of ministry together in England. Both were chosen to be interns with Christian Heritage UK in Cambridge, under Ranald Macaulay (husband of Susan Schaeffer Macaulay, author of *For the Children's Sake*). During their two-month internship, they would give tours at The Round Church, and help with the summer Christian apologetics conferences held there. They were thrilled to be venturing off to a place that had represented the zenith of their spiritual and artistic ideals for many years.

The seeds of interest were planted when we read the book *L'Abri* aloud together as a family. The story of how Frances and Edith Schaeffer started a philosophical and spiritual ministry out of their tiny chalet in Switzerland deeply impacted my kids. In their high school years, they had both delved more deeply into the Schaeffers' writings and been greatly enriched.

The ideals, personalities, and abilities of my two older children had slowly emerged through their growing-up years of travel, discussions, and experiences. Now, they were young and full of energy, and very ready for this season of their lives to test their wings. As an enthusiastic young writer, Sarah had always wanted to finish her degree at an English university where she could eventually specialize in children's literature. She had recently been accepted as one of eight-two students out of fifteen hundred who had applied at King's College in London to study towards a Master's degree in literature. Joel had always hoped to study overseas, to rub shoulders with internationals, engaging in great ideas and discussions, especially as he was our one child actually born on international soil. Both of my young adult children were brimful of dreams and growing convictions concerning the great things they hoped to do with their lives.

My children had grown much too old to be "mommied" anymore, and they were quite ready to own their own ideals, convictions, and messages as adults in their own right. I was glad. It is after all what we work for as intentional moms: children who will become whole, healthy adults who are prepared for the great spiritual work of their lives. It's what finally validates the meaning of so many years of our focused work as mothers—all the training, reading aloud, discipling, correcting, inspiring, and loving meant to prepare them to take the baton from our hands and run their own race.

But in the lead up to their leaving, our days had been caught up in much more mundane issues—last minute shopping for clothes, shoestrings, and medicine; the depositing of money into a special account; buying snack food for the apartments they would share in an effort to make their dollars stretch as far as possible. There were moments when I thought the details would never end, but the day finally came. With much ado, we managed to get the car packed, stop by the bank, and head up the Interstate to Denver International Airport to catch the overnight flight to England.

All of us had been looking forward to this moment, so I was ready, at least mentally, to release them lest they become over-ripe at home. We had planned in time on the way to airport to stop at the CHEC homeschool convention in Denver, where Clay was speaking and exhibiting our books, so the Sarah and Joel could say goodbye to their dad. As we entered the conference center, I ran into a sweet friend.

"And how is the Mama doing with her oldest children leaving together for two months? Two at once! Are you crying yet?" She gave the knowing look of a fellow mother.

My answer was probably not what she expected, but it was entirely sincere at that moment. "No. Actually, I am really ready to launch them on this trip, and I know they are really ready to go!"

I nearly added that, besides my kids obvious emotional readiness for this trip, I was very happy just to get beyond the busy-ness of the preparation. Beyond the normal responsibilities of a household full of children, all of the added support-raising, letter writing, and packing had taken its toll. It was time for all of us to move on!

I left the airport with a motherly sense of glad resignation. My friend was sweet to ask, but I felt sure I would be fine. The next few days at home I settled back into routine, rested from the last minute-craze that had surrounded the departure, and re-adjusted to a household of only two children instead of four.

That's when the absence of my older children hit me. Several days later, I was walking around the house with a hollow feeling so large in my throat I almost couldn't swallow. In the mundane moment of cleaning my bedroom, while unpacking a bag, the reality of their being away hit my heart's home. I realized that even though I was glad to see the Lord leading them on to new things, I was deeply sorry to lose the presence of those who understood, loved, and laughed with me the best. I was homesick for my children, but I knew I would just have to carry on.

The days went on, and "normal" life returned, and I began to realize just how much the absence of my two older children would change my life. In a very real sense, Clay and I had lost our best friends. There were no longer two young adults sitting up in the den until after midnight to discuss deep-soul issues, while consuming ice cream and popcorn. No longer were we getting our regular dose of new-found blogs, thought-provoking articles, and never-heard-before song debuts. Gone was my walking partner of the last twelve years who kept me entertained and enlivened in spirit with our fun and heart-felt talks as we worked to stay in shape. It simply wasn't as fun to make a cup of tea and splurge on dark chocolate all by myself.

I don't know exactly when my older children slipped out of child-at-home status, and into the friend-in-life role, but it happened quietly and without fanfare. There was so much I would miss of those childhood days, but I was also growingly grateful to God for giving me these two deeply kindred spirits when I needed them, right in my own home.

Their absence had a positive impact, too. It made me even more grateful for the extra undistracted time I could give to Joy, now my only still-young child at home. We giggled together in her bed at nights, went out for dates, drove to her many activities together, and read many of the wonderful books that had been her older siblings' favorites at her age. I also enjoyed some newfound time with Nathan. It was a grace to be able to make him a quick lunch on a break from his work, share an iced coffee with him at the local coffee shop, and chat with him about his life, friends, and future hopes and plans. Much has changed as I enter a new season with my older two gone, but there is still much to treasure.

As I consider my own life as a mother, I know how often I, and so many other moms like me, long for more time to ourselves, to have a smaller work load, and to get a little rest. It's nice to look forward to a break, and it's easy to wonder if you will ever have your old self back. But as I have passed through this season of sending out my first kids, I have seen how much the friendship of my children has replaced my need for time for my own self. I know I will not look so forward to the independence of all of my children, and the inevitable empty nest, but the reality is that in sending them into the world, I am also sending out a part of myself that can never be replaced by anyone else. That gives me satisfaction.

ﻬ

The truth is so illogical. How can I tell those sweet, young women who long for excitement, freedom, and adventure, that they will never find satisfaction of soul, or the deep knowledge that soul-mates share, by pursuing self-fulfillment. Instead, I would have to say that all the cooking, washing clothes, correcting, and sacrificing of time in a thousand different ways is the most meaningful way of building intimacy to last a lifetime. It truly is the means by which soul-deep friendships are built. Christ's exhortation that "whoever loses his life for me will find it" (Matt. 16:25) isn't simply a spiritual platitude, it is a reality. In giving up so much for so long for Christ's sake, both to my children and to my husband, I found the meaning in life and the deep relationships I had always longed for.

But it is a truth I have learned in the autumn season of motherhood. Fall is a time of changing, and the herald of new colors and experiences. It is often a time of moving on. That is how I see these transitional times of motherhood, as the fall passages of our lives. Some seasons are more about action and activity—the spring of idealism and renewal; the summer of responding to open hearts, and cultivating them for future growth. But fall is a time of change, when the leaves on the trees begin changing to red and gold, preparing to let go and fly away. We know that the ending of a season has come and that a new season is inevitably on its heels. Motherhood has its fall seasons of change, when leaves of life begin to fly away.

There are many such passages in the life of a mother, and they come whether we like them or not. It begins with the weaning of a baby from the sweet dependence of nursing to the innocence and wonder of toddlerhood. Soon after comes the newly-grown personhood of the pre-school years when a child can easily spend a night away from home without crying or clinging. After that the transitions come in rapid succession—the emergence from the elementary years, in which mom is the cherished friend, moving into the hormonal years, when a child begins exploring their God-given yearnings for independence. There are the ever-changing years of first jobs, and driver's licenses, and graduation. And then, last of all, the move into adulthood, with its claims of work and marriage, and the new reality that my home is only a place for special occasions. The precious days run so quickly away.

As I look back, I wish I had been even more intentional about enjoying each season and celebrating the joy of having these precious ones in my home. My friend reminded me of this recently when I spoke with her at a conference. As we talked, her eyes filled with tears

"I finally realized what the struggle is that has been in my heart," she said. "I finally got the point where I was enjoying my children, and their home education, and all of us being together. And now it is all changing, and we will all go our separate ways, and I don't like it at all! As a matter of fact, I hate it!"

She sighed and then continued quietly. "I am not ready, but that doesn't really matter, does it? I might as well just accept it and move on!"

I have to agree with her. I think the most difficult transition for me was the move from the elementary school years when I had my little Clarkson Club that did everything with me, to the sudden autonomy of my children's young adulthood. Before that, all of our activities were pretty much together, books were read out loud, walks were taken together, and forays into town were group trips. But suddenly, and with what seemed like not enough warning, my older kids began to pursue their own lives and activities, splitting up our little club and sending us all in differing directions. I now homeschool Joy alone, and it is a very different dynamic from that of a whole, wriggling small group of homeschooling children.

I see these seasons as times of resolve for me as a mother. I have learned that it is God's will for me to resolve, in my heart and spirit, to accept the seasons of my life as he brings them. If I fight against them, and resist simply receiving them as gifts from my gracious heavenly Father, then I will miss what God intends for me to experience from them. There is a sense of accepting the reality that life moves on, a reality Moses alluded to when he said, "Teach us to number our days aright, that we may gain a heart of wisdom" (Ps. 90:12). My days *are* "numbered," and if I resist that truth I'll miss the "wisdom" that God wants me to know.

When I resolve to accept life as God has given it, I want to do so with a grateful heart. When I entrust my precious children into God's faithful hands, I want to do so with the quiet contentment that the psalmist pictures:

"But I have stilled and quieted my soul; like a weaned child with its mother, like a weaned child is my soul within me" (Ps. 131:2). When I resolve myself to his will, and the inevitable changes that will come, it allows me to open my eyes to the joys and blessings of every day of my life. I can either resolve myself to being faithful and joyful, or I can let that opportunity pass me by. If I resolve to be faithful, I will be able to celebrate all of life as God gives it to me, without regret. I have only this one life to "do it right," and I am resolved in my heart to accept each season by faith.

If I am to meet these passages with grace, I have to cultivate a humble submission to the changes in life that God has ordained for every family, and exercise a willingness in my heart to let go and move on. I am resolving to try to go through each of these passages with the grace of acceptance. I want to release my children to God's plan for their lives with the freedom of grace. I am resolved to send them out from this, my home, with the blessing of God as they move on to the next phase in their life's adventure.

ᴥ

It is fall now, the summer internship is a memory, and both Sarah and Joel have been with me for a day by themselves up in the charming mountain town of Breckenridge. We bought a time-share many years ago when it was affordable, and have had this late fall week as an anchor around which we gather each year. We have many memories in this place—years of going to favorite cafes, watching movies together, playing games, drinking hot chocolate, and hiking around the mountain lake above our lodge. But for the past two years, our whole family has not been able to get everyone here on the same days. This year is the first time that Nathan will miss being here because of his internship with a ministry in our church. The late winds of autumn blow.

And yet, knowing that my kids are moving on has brought a special spice to our time here. It has made each meal more meaningful, each conversation more intense, and whatever we do together more worthy of celebrating as special. One night, we spent an evening in front of the fireplace talking about biblical convictions and life ideals. I sat back, observing how intelligent and authoritative my kids had become in reading and studying their own books, writing songs for albums being produced, and finishing the writing of blogs and papers. I mused about how seasoned they have become through their travels and exposure to the many people I will never meet, books I'll never read or discuss, and experiences I'll never know. Yet how precious to see before me two such fine young adults engaged in bringing light to their own generation. They are finding their own way along their journeys, and through these new passages in their own lives, and I am happy as I watch them.

Fall has come to this mother's heart. I find in this season a sense of work well done, a bright harvest being gathered in after many years of faithful, hopeful work in the fields of my children's hearts and minds. But I also find in myself a resolve to pass through this season with grace, and to find a peace as the doors of the past close behind me. I am looking ahead, by faith, to the new doors that will soon be opening on a brand new season.

❦

Fall

*Not that I have already obtained all this, or
have already been made perfect, but I press on
to take hold of that for which Christ Jesus took
hold of me.*

*Brothers, I do not consider myself yet to have
taken hold of it. But one thing I do: Forgetting
what is behind and straining toward what is
ahead,*

*I press on toward the goal to win the prize for
which God has called me heavenward in
Christ Jesus.*

Philippians 3:12-14

"A child needs sympathy hardly less than he needs love; yet ten children are loved by their parents where one child has his parents' sympathy...[It] is unquestionably true that in no way can any parent gain such power over his child for the shaping of the child's character and habits of life as by having and showing sympathy with that child."

Henry Clay Trumbull
Hints On Child Training

Chapter Seven

A Touch of Sympathy

*...clothe yourselves with compassion, kindness,
humility, gentleness and patience.*

Nathan is a good boy, as boys go. He has good days, and bad days. But in December of his fifth year, he had a bad month. Every day, it seemed, he would find a new way to get in trouble. With annoying regularity, he crossed the line from tolerable little boy excess into the out-of-control zone. While he did have his moments of obedience, decent attitudes, and self-control, they rarely came all at the same time, or even on the same day.

My maternal patience meter had, by God's grace, stayed in the acceptable range for most of that trying month. But then, when Nathan threw a wall-eyed fit one evening when his grandmother Nana was babysitting him, my emotional meter shot into and clean out of the red zone.

Of course, my own frustration had been gradually building up inside. Every time he tested my patience, I responded by becoming even more strict than I had been the last time. Somehow, I had convinced myself that this increasing harshness in discipline was the only appropriate response to his decreasing efforts at obedience. If he would not control himself, I reasoned, then I would control him.

As the parent-child hostilities escalated, I found my need to pray escalating as well. One morning, as I was pouring out my heart to God about this problem, I cried out, "Please, Lord, tell me how I should discipline Nathan! What can I do to get him to obey?" His answer was clear, but not exactly what I had expected. I felt the Spirit impress upon my heart a simple answer—spend time alone with Nathan and just let him just be himself. Hardly the strategy I had been using, or would even think of. Though I was not yet convinced, God didn't waste time in giving me an opportunity to follow his leading.

The next day, with a full house of out of town company, we decided to go out for an afternoon walk. It had turned cold, so I reminded all of the children to be sure to get their coats. To make certain he would get his coat, I repeated it to Nathan three times. He didn't get his coat.

Sure enough, when we got out into the cold December air about a half mile from home, Nathan started complaining that he was cold and couldn't go on. He wanted to go home, but no one would go with him. I was just about to sternly reprimand him with a guilt-inducing, "Didn't I tell you to get your coat?" when the Spirit of God slipped into my conscience. I felt a spiritual nudge, "Remember your prayer?"

Instead of a reprimand, I took his cold little hand in mine and spoke gently to my frustrated little boy. "I know you must be cold, sweet Nathan. Why don't you and I walk home together and get warm. I don't mind going back, and besides, I'd much rather be with you right now, anyway."

Nathan's face immediately broke out in a big smile. He grabbed my hand, kissed it and said, "You mean you'd rather be with me than all those other people? Oh, no one has a mommy like you. You are so wonderful. It makes me feel so special for you to talk with just me!" For thirty minutes, he opened up his little heart and let his feelings bubble over with me. He talked about his thoughts, he told jokes, he even shared his struggles. And all the time he talked, he continued to be affectionate and loving. He was a different child.

Over the next two weeks, I noticed a real change in Nathan's behavior and attitudes. He was still a high energy little boy, but he wasn't crossing that line any more. I could tell he was really trying to be good. The hostilities ceased. He was actually a joy to be around.

As I reflected back on the incident that seemed to have brought about his change of heart, I was reminded of a word that has kept coming up in my reading of books from the late 1800's about child-raising...sympathy. Nathan, our family's only true extravert at that time, wanted time to talk and to express all that was on his little mind and heart. In his five year-old way, he wanted to be heard and understood, and to know that someone sympathized with him. When that wasn't happening, his frustration simply expressed itself in an immature way during that December. He needed someone to get down on his level to talk with him, to feel what he felt. He needed a parent willing to show sympathy.

ও

It is so easy for me, as a parent, to become overly concerned with every jot and tittle of my children's behavior. I can spend so much time correcting them and teaching them all the right rules, that I forget the real goal of my instruction—to win their hearts for the Lord. Training and instruction alone cannot guarantee a heart for God.

If you really desire to reach your children's hearts for Christ, you cannot do so until you build a deep and trusting relationship with each child. They must feel that they can find no better confidante, no more loyal friend, no greater encourager, and no one who understands their thoughts and dreams, fears and doubts, joys and hurts better than you. And even though they understand that you want to help them grow to maturity in Christ, they must also sense that you accept them just as they are, and love them no matter what they do.

All of that comes through sympathy. And before I go further, let me be clear what I mean by the word. The word comes from Greek and literally means to "feel with." In simple terms, sympathy is simply the willingness to understand and validate your child's thoughts and feelings. It is remembering what it was like to think and feel like a child. It is not having the same feelings as your child, but rather understanding and identifying with the feelings they have. You are still the more mature parent, but your immature child knows that, and yet still feels understood.

Henry Clay Trumbull, who is Elizabeth Elliott's great-grandfather, was a nationally recognized author and leader in the American Sunday School movement in the late 1800's. After his eight children were all grown, a friend wrote and asked him what his secret was as a parent—what did he do that turned out such good children? Trumbull's now-classic book, *Hints On Child Training*, written in 1890, was his reply to his friend. It has become my favorite book on Christian parenting.

Though it sounds as if he could be speaking for our culture as well as his own, Trumbull suggested that for every ten children who are loved by their parents, only one has his parents' sympathy. He goes on to say, "It is unquestionably true that in no way can any parent gain power over his child for the shaping of the child's character and habits of life as by having and showing sympathy with that child."

Even with a flood of books and seminars on Christian parenting in our generation, we have not, it would seem to me anyway, come that far in one hundred years. Trumbull's evaluation and advice still rings true. Unless sympathy finds its place in the process of our parenting, we will be as powerless as the parents of Trumbull's day to reach and shape our children's hearts. We may succeed in raising children who follow our instructions, yet without our sympathy they may not follow our hearts. It's not that hard to force a change in outward behavior; it takes much more, though, to change a heart. Sympathy is the key that lets me into my child's heart.

I pray that God will help me, and Clay, raise our children to value our values and see with our vision for the Christian life. But if I want them to have my heart, then I must have *theirs*. Let me share a few thoughts about sympathy that have been filling my heart these days.

Accept God's choice for your child's personality

When Jesus spoke with his disciples, he affirmed them according to their strengths and drives. When seeing the strength of character within Peter, he says, "You are a rock! Upon this rock, I will build my church!" (Matt. 16:18; John 1:42). When he meets Nathanael, he affirms his straightforward personality, "Nathanael, a man in whom there is no guile!" (John 1:47). When Martha accuses Mary of being unhelpful, Jesus affirms Mary for being relationship oriented (Luke 10:42).

The first step to showing sympathy to your child is to accept and affirm the unique personality that God has given to him or her. Believe it or not, God did not give your child that personality just to help *you* grow! He gave it because he has a purpose for that child to fulfill, and he needs your child's personality strengths. God did not make a mistake in giving your child their personality, so don't make the mistake of being critical of it. Learn to appreciate God's handiwork in each of your children.

One important truth I have learned in my years of parenting is that one personality is not more spiritual than another. That may sound self-evident, but it's easy to forget. I have discovered that I tend to see the child whose personality is most like my own as more mature and spiritual than the ones whose personalities are very different from mine. Or, if a child happens to have a more compliant personality, I tend to project on them a kind of passive maturity and spirituality that isn't necessarily there. What I have had to learn to do is look through my children's personalities and into their hearts. I want to be sure I am not crediting them with more than they deserve, or less than they deserve, or missing an attitude that is covered over by a more "spiritual" personality.

I am struck by the wide range of personality gifts under our roof. One child is very competitive and self-driven. She is easy to parent and homeschool because she is self-motivated and anxious to please. She thrives on meaningful relationships. Another child is exceedingly creative, and a peacemaker-encourager. He needs help sticking to a project because he is easily distracted by dreams and creative bursts (but he draws really cute little faces on his 6's and 9's on his math papers!). Our third child is the extraverted perfectionist. However, he is our most generous child, always ready to give away a toy, or to make someone a cup of tea. He is our organizer who feels best when the house is straight and neat (Thank you, Lord!). Our latest edition is just beginning to show her personality, and it promises to be full of surprises.

Each child's personality is strong in some areas and weak in others. Each learns, decides, plays, and thinks in their own unique way. Each responds to our parental discipline and rules differently. We have learned that in order to motivate our children to want to obey us, we have to talk to them differently and discipline them differently. We don't use their personalities to excuse unacceptable behavior, but we do respond to the behavior with personality in mind. If I understand how God has "wired" each child, I can much more easily and effectively hook into the wires that take me right to that child's heart. It is the same in other areas of living and learning. I expect each child to learn differently, at their own pace and in their own way, because each has a different personality.

A sympathetic parent does not condemn or try to change a child's personality, but rather accepts each child's personality as a gift from God and guides it. Your children need to know that you accept them as God made them, not as your personality wants them to become.

Believe in your child's potential

"You always seem to talk so positively about your children! How do you do that? I only seem to see the negative sides of my children's behavior!" I appreciated that comment from a respected friend. It feels good to be believed in and affirmed.

Yet I am like anyone else—sin has left my personality with great limitations and weaknesses. And my children are no different. One of them often says, "I can't seem to be good for a whole day even if I try!" He is sensing the inadequacy that all of us as fallen sinners feel. How much more, as a child, do you think he needs to be believed in and affirmed?

Romans reminds us that while we were yet sinners, Christ died for us. He didn't wait for us to get life right. He saw within us something worth redeeming and restoring, because we were made to bear the Creator's image. He believed in us, enough to die for us, long before we ever knew to believe in him. As parents, we are called to be a picture of Christ to our children, to express our belief in them and in what they will become for God long before they themselves can see it.

I can honestly say I have never received too much encouragement from anyone. I love being around people who love me, encourage me, and think I am special. However, I studiously avoid people who always seem to have something critical or negative to say about me. The more your children sense that you believe in them, that you think they are special, the more they will want to be around you.

While that may sound like stating the obvious, it isn't always that easy to do. I think it is possible we will end up with one of each of the four personality types that we identify in our book—a Doer, a Helper, a Mover, and a Shaper (read chapter 6 in *Educating the WholeHearted Child* for profiles of each). That means that this Mover mother has to learn how to appreciate and affirm all the other personality factors that aren't like mine, and in fact are very different than mine. That does not come naturally. In order to genuinely encourage my children, I have to settle in my heart that each personality is good because it is signed "made by God," and that one personality (such as mine) is not better than others.

Ask God to show you what really drives and motivates your children. You can usually get some good clues by watching what they do when given free time without distraction. Talk to them, and try to discover their dreams. By around 12 years old the personality is fairly well settled and your child will start becoming more confident in who they are. Help them along by making observations about the strengths of their particular personality.

Envision for them ways that you see God could use them, or ways they could excel in an area of their gifts and abilities.

Then, create the opportunities that will allow them to spread their personality wings. Let them know, even at a young age, that you really believe in them and in what God is doing in their lives. Let them know that you understand their hopes, dreams, fears, and joys. With that kind of wind in their wings, you'll set them free to fly.

Learn the language of sympathy

Several years ago, one of our children went through a period of constant whining that was driving us to distraction. Our response (when we didn't just react) was usually to say something like, "I'm sorry that happened, but you need to choose to control your feelings and communicate without whining." We were so focused on the behavior that we were failing to focus on the person, an immature little boy. We were getting nowhere.

Since we'd been reading about sympathy in Trumbull, though, we thought we might as well give it a try. Nothing else was working. Our opportunity came when a prized Lego creation was destroyed by a friend. When the whining started, we sat down with him and tried the language of sympathy. "Boy, I bet that really frustrated you. If I had worked on something that special for so long, it would really make me feel bad! I'm really sorry that happened. I can understand how you feel! Now, why don't we go get a snack and some juice, and then we'll build something again later."

When the whining stopped almost immediately, we realized that much of it was just his immature way of wanting to make us feel what he was feeling. Once he knew that we understood, he lost his reason for whining. That was when we began to understand the power of sympathy.

There is a language of sympathy that is learned just like any other language. It is the words that express interest, tenderness, gentleness, confidence, loyalty, and love. Most parents know the vocabulary of the language of sympathy, but they don't get around to speaking it all that much. Like any language, you will not become fluent in it unless you speak it all the time. Express your affection, affirm their achievements, understand their disappointments, calm their fears. You cannot verbally love and appreciate your children too much.

The language of sympathy is much more than just the words, though. The verbal vocabulary of sympathy—*what* you say—is important, of course, but the *non*-verbal vocabulary—*how* you say what you say—communicates even more sympathy than the words that come out of your mouth. Eye contact, the expression on your face, your body language, and the tone of your voice are all important parts of communicating sympathy to your child. Some studies claim that as much as 90% of your message is communicated non-verbally! Maybe that's why sometimes just a hug and a smile says it all.

Whenever I really want to make sure I connect with one of my children, I engage all the tools of sympathetic communication. Before I ever say anything, I will hold a hand, kneel down, touch a shoulder, look in the eyes, exaggerate an expression, and offer a welcoming smile. Then, I use the kinds of words that will connect my heart to their hearts, and that I know will communicate to their young minds. Whenever I have an opportunity to enter into my children's world, and hopefully into their hearts, I do so intentionally, enthusiastically, and with all my senses engaged with theirs.

Make sympathy a way of life

Lest I leave the wrong impression, let me emphasize that sympathy is not just an emotional exercise of making your children feel good about you or themselves. It is how you think about your children all the time. The "I'm the parent, that's why" attitude is necessary occasionally in my parenting, but I have to be careful not to stay there. That kind of authoritarian parenting doesn't reach my children's hearts. Most of the time, my children don't need strong correction; rather, they need loving direction, and that is where sympathy comes into play.

Let me let Trumbull speak to this point. "How many parents there are...who are readier to provide playthings for their children than to share the delights of their children with those playthings; readier to set their children to knowledge-seeking, than to have a part in their children's surprises and enjoyments of knowledge-attaining; readier to make good, as far as they can, all losses to their children, than to grieve with their children over those losses. And what a loss of power to those parents as parents, is this lack of sympathy with their children as children."

What Trumbull is describing is a parent who makes sympathy a way of life, a way of seeing. It's as though we need to change eyeglasses, from the "authoritarian" style that everyone else has been wearing for so long, to the "sympathetic" style of Trumbull's day. We've lost sight of our children's hearts, and we need to adjust our vision for parenting. That's what it means to start looking at our children through the lenses of sympathy.

The mature parent knows that sympathy is not just reactive, but proactive. Sympathy is an attitude of entering into your child's life at the level where they are living it. It is a choice to leave the lofty heights of "parent" and "adult," and to come down into the world of "child." I suppose it is much like what God did for us. He left heaven and came down to our world in the ultimate, eternal act of sympathy that bought our salvation. God humbled himself to become a servant to his children.

Christ's sacrifice on the cross is such a clear picture in my mind of what it means to be a sympathetic mother. In the same way that Jesus gave up his rights to die for me, I need to give up my rights to serve my children. I need to nail my personal agenda to the cross so I can really see what my children need at any point in my day. I need to give up my tendency to want to "lord it over" them just to control them so I can accomplish my own desires. I need to humble myself so I can reach into my children's hearts without bumping into my own selfish needs and expectations. Then maybe I can be a servant to them with a heart that can sympathize with them as children. When I enter their world, only then can I truly and effectively minister to them as children. If I want to be a picture of Jesus to them, he has already sketched an outline for me. I just need to follow his example

᷾

I know I make many mistakes in mothering. Sometimes I lose my temper, sometimes I am selfish and impatient, and sometimes I am completely unaware of what is happening with my children. I sometimes think I have become so "adult" that I no longer have the capacity to really remember that I once was a child, or what it was like. I can imagine being a child, though, and not liking me as an adult all that much at times. But that's why I changed my attitude toward Nathan that cold afternoon. I wanted to be more like the kind of adult I would have felt loved by as a child. When I showed that kind of sympathy to Nathan, he forgot all of my faults and saw me as a "wonderful" person. My simple act of sympathy made him feel loved and understood.

But I want to be very clear here—I never want my sympathy to be something I "use" to get a result that I want, or only a role that I play as a parent. The author of Hebrews, who uses the Greek term for sympathy more than any other New Testament writer, said of Jesus, "we do not have a high priest who cannot sympathize with our weaknesses, but One who has been tempted in all things as we are, yet without sin" (Heb. 4:15). My role model as a sympathetic parent is Jesus, who came down to my level as a sinful human being, and *sympathized* with my lostness, weakness, and immaturity. He came down to help me, not to condemn me. That is why, the writer goes on to say, I can go to him with confidence, without fear, knowing he will help me. He knows me, and he loves me.

Jesus is the picture of a sympathetic parent. In the same way that Jesus was able "to sympathize with our weaknesses," I want to be able to sympathize, to "feel with," my children, and understand their weaknesses, uncertainties, and immaturities. Why? So they will be confident to come to me, because they know that when they do they will "receive mercy and find grace" (Heb. 4:16), just as I do when I go to Jesus.

My children are going to face so many un-sympathetic people in their lives. Even now, in their childhood, I can't control how other people speak to them, or respond to them when I'm not there. In fact, they are more likely to find indifference and harshness in other adults, and children, than they are to find sympathy. It seems to be the spirit of our age. But when they are in my home, I want them always to find a sympathetic mother who is ready at any time to listen, affirm, comfort, and guide.

We forget so many details about our growing-up years. But we remember the people, and how they related to us. And for those who loved us and understood us when we were immature children, I think we hold a special place for them in our hearts. How I hope my children remember me, in spite of everything else, as one who really knew them, understood them, loved them, and believed in them. I hope they remember feeling treasured. Perhaps then they will more quickly treasure the Christ that is in my heart, and all these years of work will have been worth the effort!

❦

Thoughts On the Living Word

We have a sympathetic God. Out of his boundless compassion and mercy, he showed sympathy for us by sending Jesus to die for our sins. Throughout Scripture, God's merciful love is cited as the model for the kind of love we are to have for him and for others. When we read those passages, we probably almost always think first of other adults receiving his sympathetic love. But what about our children? Surely God would have us love our children with the same kind of sympathetic love he commends for our adult brothers and sisters in Christ! We are the ones God has chosen through whom our children will learn of his limitless love, compassion, mercy, and forgivenss. We show them what his sympathetic, compassionate, merciful love looks like.

Matthew 9:35-38

There were certainly children in the crowds that Jesus looked upon with sympathy. When might your children feel like "sheep without a shepherd"? When your children feel "harassed and helpless," whether from circum-stances or their own sin, how is your response to them like Jesus' might have been?

Colossians 3:21

After exhorting husbands not to be harsh with their wives, Paul admonishes fathers (or, "parents") to be careful how they relate to their children. How do you, as a parent, "embitter" your children? What causes your children to become "discouraged"? What is your response to them when that happens? What role does sympathy play in your response to your children?

1 Thessalonians 2:6-12

Paul used mothers and fathers to illustrate his feelings for the Thessalonians. How does Paul compare his heart for the Thessalonians to the heart of a mother for her children? To the heart of a father for his children? In what ways are you this kind of parent with your children? What is missing in your parenting from these portraits?

Colossians 3:12-14

Paul likens the love we are to have for one another as Christians to putting on different pieces of clothing. How would your children describe the "clothing of love" they see you wearing most of the time? What pieces of clothing might be missing from your wardrobe? What does sympathy look like on you?

My Thoughts

_____

_____

_____

_____

_____

_____

_____

_____

_____

_____

_____

_____

_____

Thoughts On Living the Word

One of the easiest ways I have found to show sympathy to one of my children is to identify an area that is a delight or enjoyment to them and plan a time to participate with them in that area. With one, it might mean enjoying their music; with another, creating a Lego thing; with another, going to play tennis. ❧ To be a really sympathetic parent, I have found the most important thing I can do is study my children. I ask God to help me know their personalities, likes and dislikes, drives and discouragements. The more I understand them, the better I can sympathize with them and speak to their hearts. ❧ I have been especially encouraged recently as I have studied passages in the Gospels where Jesus related to little children. On every occasion, Jesus takes the child into his arms and blesses them in some way. He is very gentle and tender with them. I want to study more of the relational style of Jesus so I can be more like Christ with my children.

My Life

Personal application: Study your children this week. With Colossians 3:21 in mind, think about each individual child. Try to determine how the way you relate to them might frustrate them and discourage them. Plan a positive way to change that relational pattern.

Family application: Create a questionnaire that probes likes and dislikes, preferences for living and learning, and hopes and dreams. Make copies and personally interview each child with the questions. Summarize any discoveries you make about their personalities.

"God never insists on our obedience; human authority does. Our Lord does not give us rules and regulations; He makes very clear what the standard is, and if the relation of my spirit to Him is that of love, I will do all He wants me to do without the slightest hesitation. If I begin to object, it is because I love someone else in competition with Him, namely, myself."

Oswald Chambers
He Shall Glorify Me

Chapter Eight

Freedom from Guilt

Since we live by the Spirit, let us keep in step
with the Spirit. Let us not become conceited,
provoking and enying one another.

W ith just a few casual words, my friend inadvertently neutralized the Christmas cheer I was feeling. It had been a huge effort over the previous two months to get moved and settled into our new house in Fort Worth. Having a Christmas open house was like saying, "You can look now." After the weeks of disorganization and disarray, I was feeling pretty good about how much I'd accomplished, even with my quick fix of putting all the leftovers in our bedroom. I was pleased to be able to open my house and entertain others during my favorite season of the year. Whatever good feelings I had been feeling, though, soon unraveled with my friend's words. Let me back up a couple of months, though, to put the unraveling in context.

It was November 1, our first day in the new house in Fort Worth, and I was officially under the pile—surrounded by boxes, messes, stuff, empty cabinets, and empty walls. We'd moved a lot of times before, so it wasn't that I didn't know where to begin or what to do. It's just that I was already feeling overwhelmed from an incredibly busy September and October—

three out-of-town ministry trips, every Friday and Saturday night performing in *The Promise* with the children until midnight, looking for and buying the house, regular 120-mile round-trip jaunts to Fort Worth, all on top of the myriad of "normal" homeschooling mother responsibilities. I felt like a winded runner holding my sides and gasping for breath. But I couldn't stop running yet. Thanksgiving was coming.

We organized the kitchen, put up the beds, unloaded all the children's toys and games (to keep them busy!), filled the cabinets with sheets and towels, distributed boxes, organized the garage (sort of), and cleaned up the yard. We also had to shop for new furniture to fill in gaps in several rooms, find bookcases for our growing library of beloved books that languished in boxes, arrange for some new kitchen appliances, and fix a few things. Throughout the month we slowly but steadily put up pictures, and decorated the living room, dining room, and den.

We were still panting when Thanksgiving came, and with it a full house of fourteen family members. It was a wonderful family celebration, complete with a very fat turkey, squash casserole, homemade rolls, pumpkin pie, and lots of leftovers. The main living areas were relatively uncluttered and festively decorated for the fall. Everyone talked and talked, and warm memories were put away in my children's minds. Did someone say... Christmas?

The Thanksgiving dishes were no sooner done than I found myself facing December. One more deep breath and off we went again. Of course, we continued the organization process of putting books on shelves, setting up computers and the home learning room, and dealing with moving details. But we also dug out the Christmas decorations from the not-yet-so-organized garage, and plunged headlong into the task of decorating the house for our first Christmas there. The children insisted on keeping all our Christmas traditions alive in the new house, but especially our traditional Christmas open house.

I love entertaining, so I was really pleased with how everything looked on the day of the open house. The living areas were decorated with bright greens and reds of Christmas, a table full of lovingly prepared Christmas delicasies greeted our guests, the lighted candles and the fire in the fireplace added a warmth to the room, and the melodies of familiar Christmas music filled the room. It was such a lovely festive atmosphere that it made me forget all about our bedroom in the back stacked floor-to-ceiling with all the leftover stuff that had cluttered the house.

All went well with the open house until a small group of friends reminded me of the one room that wasn't quite yet done. They asked, "Can we sneak back to see the rest of the house?" What could I say but, "Sure, as long as you promise to overlook the piles that we haven't gotten to yet!" I gave them a guided tour down the hallway. They were admiring the sweet home the Lord had provided for our family when we finally reached my overloaded bedroom. Someone commented how nice and large our bedroom was, and then it happened. The unraveling began.

One of my friends casually commented that when she had moved into her house an older woman had given her some advice. This woman said that if you really love your husband, and want to show him that he has first priority in your life, then you will make your bedroom the first place you organize and decorate. Ouch! That one simple comment cut straight to my heart and pierced it. She was right! It was obvious I had not paid any attention to our bedroom. I hadn't been thinking of Clay at all, only myself and getting my home in order.

I felt a deep stab of guilt as I realized how I surely must have disappointed my dear husband over the past two months. I had labored so hard to make my house nice, yet I had neglected his needs. What must he think of me? Why hadn't I seen what I was doing? I felt like the wind had been knocked out of me. Whatever good feelings I had about my new home started to unravel within me. After several days of feeling heavy-hearted and discouraged, I decided to tell Clay how sorry I was that I had not been a better wife.

I brewed him a cup of his favorite tea and sat down with him on the couch. I reviewed the past two months, then explained what my friend had said and how it had cut me to the heart. I apologized to him for not being more sensitive to him, and for neglecting our bedroom for so long. I promised I would give it my highest priority immediately. I waited for a reply that would confirm my concerns.

Clay looked at me with a puzzled expression and said, "What in the world are you talking about?" I thought maybe he didn't understand how I had offended him so I explained it all again. He touched my shoulder and very matter-of-factly said, "Honey, it doesn't bother me at all that our bedroom is a mess. What's important to me is to have the main areas of the house neat and orderly. When they feel settled and homey, then I feel good about life. We only see the bedroom when we go to bed and get up, but we live most of our lives in the rest of the house. I really appreciate everything you've done to turn this house into our home. I know we'll get to the bedroom eventually. You've done a great job!"

I felt an immediate sense of relief from the guilt I had been feeling. But that was followed by an equal measure of indignation as I realized what had happened to me. Without even knowing it, I had judged myself guilty by someone else's standard. I had condemned myself by that standard and was left feeling like a complete failure. To my family and loved ones I was doing just fine, yet I was blinded to that fact by my own self-induced guilt.

As I reflected on what had happened I could see that what my friend had said was not necessarily wrong, and that it did have some wisdom to it. But I could also see that what she said was not a biblical standard. It was just someone's opinion, not a divine regulation or universal rule. And what may have been relevant for someone else was not relevant to my situation. I had taken it in because it "sounded" good, but had not stopped to discern whether or not it was a biblical standard. In my moment of weakness, I condemned myself unnecessarily.

I was struck by how easily I, as a reasonably mature Christian, could fall victim to that kind of false guilt. It makes me wonder how many other well-intentioned mothers are unthinkingly binding themselves to man-made rules and standards that put them under a load of guilt. The message of the New Testament is that there is now "no condemnation" for those who are in Christ, and that we have been "freed from the Law." Yet I worry that the freedom and grace that we have in the Lord is being subtly supplanted by man-made rules and regulations.

❧

When Clay and I decided to homeschool, we were attracted to it because we felt it was the very best way to raise our children in the training and instruction of the Lord. Conventional schooling, whether public or private, would remove them from our influence during the most formative years of their lives. We wanted to be the ones to shape our children's hearts for God, to fill their minds with truth, and to pass along to them a Christian heritage that would carry over into future generations. We just couldn't imagine giving up those privileges to someone else.

Our vision for the homeschooling lifestyle, at first, was simple, pure, and unadulterated. We were bolstered in our decision by the unity we felt with other homeschoolers when the movement was still relatively new. There was a "we're all in this together" mentality that undergirded our new lifestyle. A decade later, though, I am amazed at how complicated and confusing that choice has become. I don't think it is because homeschooling has changed, but I'm afraid the homeschooling movement has. The homeschooling community is beginning to resemble the church at Corinth. Wherever homeschoolers gather, you begin to hear "I am of this method of homeschooling," or "I am of this authoritative teacher," or "I am of this movement or group," or "I am of this historical tradition." What used to be simply the decision to homeschool, has become a decision of *how* to homeschool.

There is literally a smorgasbord of homeschooling philosophies and methods to choose from, each with its own standards and goals. As the variety and number of approaches increases with each year, I have observed that the standards keep getting raised higher and the rules defined more sharply in order to safeguard the quality and uniqueness of each approach. In the zeal to set one approach apart from the others, some will say that their way is the best way, even God's way. Many mothers who accept such an argument, though, soon find that the freedom and joy of doing God's will their way with their children has been subtly supplanted by the burden of trying to do God's will someone else's way.

Speakers also often point to their own children as examples to convince you that their way to homeschool is the right way—they score at the 99th percentile on achievement tests, have sterling character, work without complaint, and always do more than is required! And since you know *your* children aren't that way, you begin to wonder if you're doing enough, or if maybe your children could be like the speaker's if you used that method. And it's the same whether they are keynote speakers at a large convention, or just workshop leaders promoting different methods of teaching reading, math, or language arts, or why your children need Greek and Latin while they are young, or how they should study the Bible. And then there are all the character training and lifestyle issues that creep into the academic mix— clothing choices, food and nutritional convictions, "homesteading" skills, music preferences, and on and on. Whatever happened to simply homeschooling!?

It's still there, of course, but it just isn't quite as simple as it used to be. There are so many good speakers to learn from now, and generally they are up there speaking because they have high ideals and high standards of excellence, so it's natural for each one to want to think their way is the "high standard" for home education. I speak from experience as a national speaker because reaching for the higher ideals and the pursuit of excellence is what drives my messages (I personally would not come to hear me speak if I thought all I would hear was low ideals and mushy standards). How- ever, if guilt becomes the motivation for choosing an approach, whether because it is implied that what you are doing isn't good enough, or because you should want only the very best, then the standard has been lowered not raised. I fear that I, too, have been guilty of subtly communicating that kind of guilt when what I really wanted to do was set my listeners free to follow God in their home and family.

Because it is a "Christian" homeschooling movement, it is natural for highly idealistic and committed speakers to subtly promote their own standards as God's truth without even realizing it. Someone might imply that God has provided a "formula" that, if followed, carries the promise of God's blessing. The formula is often based on biblical principles rather than on direct biblical teaching, but it still carries a claim of biblical authority.

I see a trend in the homeschool movement of appealing to homeschooling parents based on the belief that there is a "formula" that will make them successful, whether in academics, character training, or lifestyle. Sometimes that mentality is intentionally created and fostered. Most of the time, though, it is unintentionally created and reinforced by well-intentioned speakers who suggest that homeschooling is as easy as following their particular educational approach.

Whatever the source, when Christian homeschoolers begin to rely more on formulas, and less on faith in God, then they are not reaching for a higher standard. It is an unfortunate development if our reliance on God for our children's development is weakened by our immature or unconfident need to depend on someone else's formula. What is even worse, though, is if the formula becomes a standard by which others' lives are evaluated or judged. It is a very short step from standing firm on high ideals and standards to what I would call practicing "Christian law."

Many matters of Christian faith and practice find their origin in specific scriptures, but are in reality man-made standards. For instance, God's word admonishes women to dress modestly, which is clearly a biblical principle. If, however, a teacher says that all Christian women should wear only white garments as symbolic of their godly purity, that is no longer biblical principle but a man-made standard. It is a formula for how you can be sure to obey the principle. God has provided very few such formulas in Scripture; rather, he encourages us to live by faith, not depending on formulas to know if we are "doing it right," but on Christ, and on the Spirit of God in our hearts.

Unfortunately, the urge to create or live by Christian law, by formula, runs deep within us. If I think I am right about something, whether it be about education, parenting, Christian lifestyle, or whatever, there is something deep within me (and within every other believer) that wants everyone else to agree with me, not just in principle, but in practice. If I use my personal standard to judge another person's standards, then I have created Christian law. And when it is used even to accuse others, or to question their relationship with God, then it becomes legalism, a sin for which Jesus reserved some of his harshest rebukes.

Legalism is the practice of creating external standards of belief or behavior to judge whether a person is righteous, or mature, or not. The Law was an *external* standard, but it could never save anyone, or make anyone righteous. Paul made clear that the Law, though good, was only a "tutor" that would reveal our sin and show us our need for a Savior. The gospel, though, is an *internal* standard. It is the good news that God has graciously provided a Savior, and we can be accepted by God by faith alone in what he did for us on the cross. Our external works are worthless to earn his favor; all he requires is our internal faith.

The apostle John wrote about Jesus, "For the Law was given through Moses; grace and truth were realized through Jesus Christ" (Jn.1:17). He is contrasting them, and letting us know that Jesus came to set us free from the burden of the Law, and to enable us to live instead by "grace and truth." That's good news...that's the gospel! And yet, Christians can still give in to the urge to externalize grace and truth into Christian law. Grace can be externalized into a legalism of behavior—be like me to be acceptable (follow my rules about activities, associations, food, clothes, music, media, etc.). Truth can be externalized into a legalism of belief—believe like me to be acceptable (accept my doctrines, my belief about church, my rules about men and women, my beliefs about eschatology, etc.). Christ gave us his Holy Spirit so we could live by faith, with grace and truth in balance.

Paul rebuked and corrected the Galatian church for trying to impose external legal standards of behavior and belief on new Christians. "It was for freedom that Christ set us free; therefore keep standing firm and do not be subject again to a yoke of slavery" (Gal. 5:1).He told them that those who imposed law on the gospel were living by the flesh. In other words, they were out of fellowship with God. Instead, he said, we are to live "by the Spirit," from the inside out, for "if you are led by the Spirit, you are not under the Law" (Gal. 5:18). Either we live by grace, or we live by law.

There is no law that can create God's spiritual fruit in our lives. It comes only from the Spirit of God in our hearts, as we let him live through us. "But the fruit of the Spirit is love, joy, peace, patience, kindness, goodness, faithfulness, gentleness and self-control. Against such things there is no law" (Gal. 5:22-23, NASB). We cannot live the Christian life on our own; we live the Christian life only as we walk in the power of the Holy Spirit. The good news is that you are free in Christ, and do not need to be under the Law, or under the yoke of someone's Christian law.

ॐ

When I think of the truths of Scripture that have influenced me most, especially in the New Testament, I think of the Apostle Paul's admonition that "we live by faith, not by sight" (2 Cor. 5:7). God makes it clear, especially through the writings of Paul, that we have been set free from the rule of law (living by "sight"), in order to live by faith, in the power of the Holy Spirit. A formulaic faith is no faith at all, but just rule-keeping that can become little more than self-righteousness. God wants us to live by faith in Christ, instructed by his word, and guided by his Holy Spirit, not in an immature dependence upon others to tell us how to live. He wants us to live by faith, in mature dependence upon him for the wisdom that he "gives generously to all without finding fault" (James 1:5).

That wisdom will come from more than just my own individual study of the Bible and walk with Christ. I am always learning more from my husband, teachers, pastors, writers, books, articles, tapes, radio, and more. The body of Christ, whether in its local or universal expression, is a continuous source of God's wisdom. Ultimately, though, I alone will have to answer to God for my stewardship of that wisdom. Freedom comes not from depending upon someone else's wisdom, but from following the Spirit's leading into my own convictions that guide the decisions and allegiances of my heart. I cannot let someone else walk by faith for me. I must walk by faith.

The more I study it, the more this principle jumps off the pages of my Bible. I personally need to keep my mind renewed with this truth of God's word so I don't subtly fall into the trap of thinking I need a formula to please God, or worse, begin to suggest that others do. Living by faith is not a life of formula, but a life of freedom. I want to be sure I'm living in that freedom and offering it to others.

Paul had to correct the church in Rome, too. Some Jews who were becoming Christians felt they still needed to observe some of the Jewish dietary laws, and the Sabbath, and similar rules. In their case, Paul had to correct the "strong" (mature) Christians, who had found freedom from the Law, not to abuse their freedom by flaunting it before those who were "weak." The principle that Paul teaches guides us still today, 2,000 years later: "The faith which you have, have as your own conviction before God. Happy is he who does not condemn himself in what he approves" (Rom. 14:22, NASB). In other words, you are free to live by the Spirit.

❧

It deeply concerns me when we receive letters from homeschooling mothers who, in addition to feeling overwhelmed and tired, are emotionally drained by the sense of judgment and condemnation they feel from their own support groups. One woman told me how she had told her friends that she was feeling overwhelmed and depressed, and was concerned that her children didn't measure up to their peers. Rather than finding help or encouragement, her attitudes were cooly labeled as sin that needed to be confessed. I, too, fall into "sinful" attitudes at times, but what I need at those times is a friend, not a judge. I need to be reminded of the freedom I have in Christ, of the power of the Holy Spirit to live joyously, of the provisions of a gracious and loving Father in the midst of trials.

Many mothers handle the pressure of homeschooling just fine, but more than we care to admit do not. Several very special homeschooling friends of mine have quietly and privately had nervous breakdowns—not just bad days, but emotional incapacitation. Where there is freedom in Christ and life in the Spirit, this should not be happening with such regularity. If homeschooling is indeed God's will for our lives, then it is "good, and acceptable, and perfect" (Rom. 12:2, NASB). Homeschooling should be a blessing to us, not an unbearable burden. If it is such a burden, then perhaps we have required things of ourselves that the Lord never asked us to do. Perhaps the standards we are trying to follow are not God's standards, but man's. Perhaps we are living by formula, rather than by faith.

What we need in our journey of homeschooling is not judgment and condemnation when we are down, but encouragement, help, affirmation and prayer to raise us up. Just by our decision to homeschool we already face a bevy of critics—other parents who vocally defend public schools for their children, church members who think we're too overprotective, family members who think we've gone off the deep end, and neighbors who suspect us of something weird but they're just not sure what. And as if that weren't enough, we add our own voices to the critics' chorus, berating ourselves that we aren't doing enough and feeling like a failure because we don't live up to the unreasonable demands we place on ourselves. Sometimes that is because of our own insecurity, immaturity, or limitations. Sometimes it is because we fail to discern that a teaching is not a biblical standard, but just someone's opinion. Sometimes it is because we have willingly put ourselves under the rule of a "Christian law."

Whatever burden you may carry, my one desire is that you would find freedom in the Spirit to follow Christ—freedom to do God's will your way in your home. I have in the past wrongly wanted others to do God's will my way, or I have judged others harshly by my own idealistic standards. Thankfully, God humbled me and renewed my thinking. The more I have discovered the grace and freedom of Christ as a homeschooling mother, the more I have wanted to offer it to others. The more I have been freed to love him and serve him in my home, the more I have wanted to encourage others to do the same.

"Therefore there is now no condemnation for those who are in Christ Jesus. For the law of the Spirit of life in Christ Jesus has set you free from the law of sin and of death" (Rom. 8:1-2, NASB).

❧

Thoughts On the Living Word

In *A Pilgrim's Progress*, the classic allegory by John Bunyan, Christian carries a heavy burden on his back until he comes to the cross. There, the burden falls off his back and rolls down the hill, never to be seen again. Like Christian, we lost the burden of our sin and guilt at the cross. Yet even after experiencing the freedom of forgiveness, we seem eager to pick up new burdens of guilt created by ourselves or others. We try to carry around man-made rules and regulations because we have been told they will enable us to please God. It is a heavy and unnecessary burden to carry. God is pleased when we simply live by faith, in the power of the Holy Spirit, in the freedom we found at the cross. When we are free of burdens, we are free to keep in step with the liberating life of the Holy Spirit.

Galatians 5:13-26

Some Galatians were trying to say Christians still had to obey the Law, but Paul tells them they are free in Christ. What does it mean to be "called to be free"? How is love different from law? How is living "by the Spirit" different from living "under law"? How does the "fruit of the Spirit" relate to our freedom in Christ?

Colossians 2:16-23

Paul wrote to correct false teaching in Colossae. What "human commands and teachings" have you seen that could keep a Christian from living by faith? What kinds of teaching today have the "appearance of wisdom" but are ineffective? What happens to you when you accept the "judgment" of another person about how you live as a Christian?

Romans 14:13-23

Paul talks about the freedom we have as Christians, but also the responsibility that goes along with it. How does "passing judgment" on another person create a "stumbling block" in their way? When is it not right to exercise our freedom in Christ? What makes a man "blessed" in verse 22? What do you "approve" that others might not?

Romans 8:1-4

Paul contrasts life under the Law with the life of the Spirit. What is it that has set us free as Christians and removed all condemnation from us? What did Jesus do that the Law could not? How can we fulfill the "righteous requirements of the law" by living in the Spirit? Do you ever find yourself wanting law to live by or law to enforce?

My Thoughts

Thoughts On Living the Word

I still remember the first time I cleansed my heart with the "spiritual soap" of 1 John 1:9. I wrote down on a sheet of paper any known sins in my life, including areas of self-condemnation, judgment, or failure. Then I wrote "1 John 1:9" across the sheet in large letters. Finally, I wadded it up and threw it away, claiming the forgiveness and freedom of Christ. ❧ If I have felt burdened by false guilt, I know others have, too. When I notice a friend might be discouraged, I'll meet them for breakfast or invite them over for lunch or tea with the intention of ministering to them and praying for them. I might also send a card with an encouraging note and a meaningful scripture. ❧ I have to take time to evaluate occasionally to see if my parenting style or discipline has relied on any guilt-inducing methods. If I have wrongly created false guilt or unnecessary burdens in my children's consciences, I need to counteract that with a double-strength dose of forgiveness, grace, and freedom.

My Life

Personal application: In your quiet time this week, ask God to show you any burdens of guilt you may be trying to carry unnecessarily. Whatever their source, use the 1 John 1:9 exercise above to cleanse your heart and give you a fresh, clean start on living by faith.

Family application: Plan a "grace day" for your homeschooling routine. Rather than telling them what to study and learn, let them decide for that day what they would like to do. It still needs to be homeschooling, but give them the freedom to set the learning agenda that day.

"Yet Christian teaching, for all its worth, is only half the story. Our real values, the way we live, must be congruent with the Christian message we espouse. Inevitably, our 'informal currciulum,' what we teach by our behavior, speaks louder than our 'formal curriculum,' the message we articulate."

Stacy & Paula Rinehart
Living in the Light of Eternity

Chapter Nine

Living with Discipleship

*Love one another...By this all men will know
that you are my disciples, if you love one
another.*

Bubbling over with the childish excitement that only Christmas can bring, two year-old Joy looked over at me in the car and nearly shouted with glee, "Mommy, they are playing my song!" Her song, of course, was *Joy to the World*. The song, and her name, seemed so appropriate for this joyful fourth child. She was our unexpected bundle of joy after three miscarriages and well into my forties.

With each of my children, I could begin to sense what they would be like even while they were still in my womb. Joy, though, was more of a mystery. Perhaps she was more content to "enjoy the ride" in my womb, taking in whatever I was doing. I've often wondered how much her personality might have been shaped by her early experiences on the stage of *The Promise*, the dramatic musical of the life of Christ in which we performed for several years. She was arguably the youngest actor on the amphitheater stage as I played my parts in numerous scenes every weekend with her going everywhere with me inside my womb. She even took a ten-day trip with me to Moscow, Russia during her fourth month in the womb and "appeared" on stage at the Kremlin Palace Theater. After the seasonal hiatus, we were back in rehearsals for the new season during her last two months in the womb.

Two days after Joy was born, she was on stage opening night with me in my arms, comfortably riding like a good Hebrew baby might have in a shoulder sling. She was there forty more nights with me throughout that season, on stage with over one hundred other cast members acting and singing their hearts out. In between scenes and during the intermission, she would lie in her baby seat backstage as other actors in the cast and crew would come by to smile at her, singing or humming the familiar tunes we had just been singing on stage, nearly enfolding her in their colorful costumes as they leaned over her for a closer look. After the seasonal break, her world was filled once again as the next season kicked in with tryouts, rehearsals, and forty more performances on stage in my arms. This time, she got to see me playing the part of older Mary at the cross, and singing a duet with John. Even Jesus himself would come by every night during the Sermon on the Mount scene, look her in the eyes, and caress her sweet face.

The effects of all this stage experience has been very pronounced. By the time she was fifteen months old, she had learned on her own to use her baby blanket as a shawl, like the women on stage, and she would dance around the living room singing "He is Je-ho-ba." Whenever she heard music playing on the stereo from the nativity scene in *The Promise*, she would stop what she was doing and make a low bow to honor the newborn Jesus. Soon, she began asking for *The Promise* music at night as she went to bed, and to watch the video during the day. At two-and-a-half, over a year after we quit the show, she would still regularly wrap her blanket around her head as a covering and go around the house calling herself "Mary," her brother "my Joseph," and her baby dolls "Jesus."

What I find interesting as we have watched our "little Mary" act out her parts is that we never made any formal attempts to teach her the songs, or to show her how to dress, or to teach her the movements we made during each song. Whatever she learned was simply been absorbed from being with us as we learned and performed our parts for the production. She heard the instructions we received from our director, she sensed the dramatic expression that we would add to our lines and acting, she picked up the joy and excitement that all of us felt in our performances, and she took in the moods and messages of each song. We never purposefully taught her, yet she was learning the whole time.

ᛘ

As I was thinking about discipleship for this chapter, it dawned on me that our experience with Joy and *The Promise* is a kind of living illustration of what it means to disciple our children. Discipleship is not just a formal, step-by-step procedure that our children must perform; it is a natural, relational, learning process, as natural as Joy learning from her experiences with us. She had been surrounded by people who acted in and loved *The Promise*, and who loved her. We all talked about it, practiced it, performed it, listened to it, and sang it. It was natural for Joy to love what we loved because we loved her. She loved *The Promise* because she loved us and was a part of our lives. That, in its essence, is what discipleship at home should be—our children loving the Jesus we love because we love them.

Most of us probably chose to begin homeschooling not for purely educational concerns, but primarily for spiritual ones. Our deepest desire and motivation was, and is, to nurture in our children a heart for God. We want them to follow the Jesus we follow, to share our faith, to believe our Bible, to value what we value, and to imitate our lives. By starting them well on that path in childhood, our hope is to see them become mature Christians as adults. That's what the Proverb means: "Train a child in the way he should go, and when he is old he will not turn from it" (Prov. 22:6). To paraphrase, it is to start a child walking on the path of righteousness while the child is still young. Then, as the Proverb goes on to say, when he is older he will remain on that path. That is a clear picture of what it means to "disciple" your child; that is, to make him a follower Jesus.

What we soon discover, though, is that there is very little in Scripture about how to raise young children to be disciples of Jesus. We certainly know that we are to "bring them up in the training and instruction of the Lord," (Eph. 6:4, NASB), and we know Deuteronomy 6:4-9 about teaching God's truth to our children in the midst of daily life, and we know a few other similarly general admonitions. However, even though these passages contain some of the language of discipleship, the instructional outline is relatively empty when it gets down to the real "how to" level of making disciples of our young children. God simply has not provided specific instructions or commands in the Bible that tell us exactly what to do, what to teach, what to train, what to correct, or even when to do it. Apparently, God trusts Christian parents to do what needs to be done, without having to tell them exactly what to do. However, it seems we don't always trust ourselves as much as God does.

So, we begin to try to fill in the blanks of the biblical outline. We look for materials that others have created to help us do what God has told us to do with our children. We sift and sort through a mountain of books, Bibles, Bible studies, periodicals, curricula, software, and other resources designed for parents to use with their children. Eventually, we filter out all but the very few that aren't too childish, too demanding, too advanced, or too expensive. At some point, we decide which resource will best enable us to disciple our children. And without even realizing it, we have fallen into a subtle trap. We become dependent upon someone or something else to tell us how to do what God has told us to do. We begin depending on books and materials to do the work of discipleship for us, rather than depending on God to help us do the work of discipleship with our children. In that process, I am afraid we are in danger of losing sight of the true essence of discipleship, especially as it works within a family unit.

If that happens, though, it may be because we have never stopped long enough to grapple with what discipleship should look like in our own family. We may all use the same word, but discipleship can mean very different things to different people. After all, there is no specific biblical definition of "discipleship." It is, rather, a New Testament concept that is defined by the scriptures you choose to apply to it. To one, it may be a very formal process of one-on-one training and instruction; to another, it may be an informal process of living and learning together; to another, it may be both; to another, something else altogether.

I believe, though, that there are some core qualities of biblical discipleship that are true of every expression of it, no matter how it gets fleshed out in real life. The qualities are more mindset than method, but it is a mindset that requires action. If you get them right, no matter what else you do or don't do, discipleship will be happening in your home. I want to explore three qualities that are at the heart of what I would call true biblical discipleship, especially as they relate to your role as a mother.

Discipleship requires a personal relationship

Even though we would deny it, we sometimes live as though we believe that being related is the same as having a relationship. Of course that's not true, we say, but do our lives always confirm that denial? We can love our children dearly, teach them diligently, train them effectively, live with them day-in and day-out, and yet still not really have a relationship with them. We can occupy the same space with them in our home, yet fail to fill the relational space between their hearts and ours. The first core quality of discipleship is a personal relationship. Without it, biblical discipleship is not going to happen in your home with your children.

When I speak of personal relationship with my children, what I mean is a relationship that can move at any time from facts and details, to faith and feelings. We can move from the surface issues to the deeper issues without hindrance. Yes, I know, my children are still developing emotionally and spiritually, but part of their maturing process is learning very early on to be honest and open about what they're feeling and what they are really thinking. I never underestimate the depth of my children's thoughts, fears, perceptions, and insights. I work at my personal relationship with them to fill that space between our hearts with openness and understanding, with a freedom to talk about any thing at any time, and with a vulnerability on my part as a mother. Those are the things that make relationship personal.

The life of Jesus is a wonderful picture of the priority of personal relationship in the process of discipleship. Jesus chose his disciples to be "with him" at all times. They literally "followed" him everywhere he would go (the word disciple in Greek means a "follower" or "learner"). Throughout the three years they were together, Jesus related to his disciples at an emotional, spiritual level. He would talk about their faith, their fears, their thoughts, and their misunderstandings. This quality is especially clear in Jesus' final days before his crucifixion. In the Garden of Gethsemane, they saw his heart open before them. After his resurrection, he is tender and open with his fearful friends. When Jesus ascended to heaven, these men were left with more than a body of teaching, they were left with the memory of a deep, personal relationship with the Son of God. He was not just a concept, but a loving, laughing, weeping, caring Messiah who opened his heart to them as no one had ever done before.

On the night that he would die, Jesus had gathered his twelve disciples in an upper room for a last meal, to share his heart with them, and to pray for them. At the top of his list of things that he wanted to say before he left them was a "new commandment." He said, "Love one another. As I have loved you, so you must love one another" (Jn. 13:34). Personal relationship was first on his heart at the last. But even more telling is what he said next. "By this all men will know that you are my disciples, if you love one another" (Jn. 13:35)Loving, personal relationship would be the mark of true discipleship.

I am convinced that God has built into the mother and child relationship much of the same dynamic that was in the relationship between Jesus and his disciples. By God's design, your children are meant to be "with you." All the elements for a deep personal relationship are already in place—the bond of love, the nurturing, comforting, and training, and the togetherness. God seems to have designed you as a mother to be your child's first and foremost arena of relationship. If you accept that design and channel your heart into that personal relationship with your child, you are taking the first and most important step toward turning your child into a disciple. If they learn the patterns of relationship from you, it will be an easier step for them to relate to Jesus.

Discipleship requires a spiritual intent

There are two kinds of Christian parents. One kind lives what I would call an unintentional Christian life. They may go to church, have their children in Bible Club, and fellowship with other Christian families. They may even homeschool their children. They do lots of good things, but only because they are good things to do, not because they are the best things to do. The other kind of Christian parent lives what I would call an intentional Christian life. They start with a spiritual intent, that they want to disciple their children to become followers of Jesus Christ. As they look at the good things to do, they choose the ones that fit their spiritual intentions for their children. Nothing is done accidentally or incidentally. What they choose to do, they do on purpose, intentionally, because it is the best thing for their children.

Spiritual intent can lead a family to make a decision that to others, or to the world, might seem misguided, or even foolish. We recently had Joel audition for an internationally recognized touring musical group for boys. Our intent was to give him an opportunity to use his obvious musical gifts. We weren't prepared for the director's effusive admiration of Joel's vocal skill, and his insistence that Joel was the best audition he had ever had. Although he wanted us to let Joel join the international touring group, we had to say no since he would have to be in their private school with all the other boys. Even though it was only ten minutes away, our spiritual intentions for his life precluded such an arrangement, so we let him join and participate in the smaller group that sang locally and sometimes with the touring group.

After a semester, though, it was evident that there were some good reasons that this was not a good situation for Joel. Despite the excellent musical training and opportunities he enjoyed, we became concerned with some issues that were in conflict with our values and standards. Because we had a spiritual intent for how to raise Joel, though, it enabled us to make a decision that others might not understand. And sure enough, several people challenged us, saying we were robbing Joel of a once-in-a-lifetime opportunity. But because we knew our intent for him, we also knew it would be much worse for us to rob him of his once-in-a-lifetime opportunity to have a full childhood at home, in our family.

Jesus certainly had to make intentional decisions about the limited time he had to prepare his disciples for ministry. In just three short years, he would place God's mission for the world into their hands. It is clear in Scripture that he was intentional about three spiritual priorities—training them to minister, teaching them his truth, and modeling his life. He was preparing the soil of their hearts for the Holy Spirit who would empower them to take over where he would leave off. All of his actions, words, attitudes, and relationships were spiritually intentional—he was preparing his disciples to be the leaders of his church. And when the end came, Jesus could say with full confidence that he had accomplished all the Father sent him to do (Jn. 14:16-17).

I can't help but see a similarity to Jesus' ministry with his disciples in my ministry of discipleship with my children. I have a very short time, just a few years, to prepare them to take over where I leave off as a mother, and where Clay and I leave off as parents. Unless I am intentional in how I make use of the years of childhood, I will miss the opportunity. The windows of their hearts begin to close when they move into young adulthood, so I have only the time until they are about 12 years old to accomplish in their lives the task of raising them to be disciples of Jesus Christ. Only a thoroughly thought through spiritual intent will help ensure that I reach the end of their childhood with confidence that I have done what God wanted me to do.

The reality is, though, I am a homeschooling mother—always busy, always needed, always wanted, daily battling an endless list of chores to be done, constantly caring for a family that insists on eating meals and wearing clean clothes, and learning to live with sleep deprivation and chronic tiredness. All that to say, it is not always easy to live with spiritual intent for all my children. It's easier, sometimes, to tell myself, "We did our devotions, we go to church, they memorize Scripture. That's all they need. I've done enough!" But it's not enough. What they really need is my life, my heart, my touch, my love, my patience, my correction, my gentleness, and my encouragement. They need me there during the many teachable moments of each day, turning them into discipling moments because my of my spiritual intent for their lives.

Discipleship requires a living example

One cool and overcast fall afternoon, we decided it was still worth it to pack a picnic lunch and head over to the play area at a large city park. Clay, the boys, and Joy were off climbing on the playground equipment as I was cleaning up our picnic site. I had noticed earlier a scraggly looking middle-aged man, surrounded by several grocery bags, sitting alone on one of the play area benches. It was obvious he was a drifter of some kind, probably a homeless man. As I looked at him I felt moved by the Spirit to offer him a leftover sandwich, some chips and fruit. He was very pleasant when I walked over to ask him if he would like some of our food. He thanked me for my small offering, packed his bags, and headed to a picnic table in an adjoining area.

Sarah, who had observed this exchange, was moved by my example and decided she wanted to give the man five dollars. I checked with Clay, who was back with the baby, and he felt it would be alright. So Sarah and I walked over to the man's table to visit with him. I asked about his life, told him about ours, and then tried to share a little about the love and forgiveness I had found in Christ. He was shy, but responsive, and told us about the guilt he had been carrying for years. I tried to minister a little more, but I could sense we had fulfilled our ministry. Sarah gave him her five dollars, for which he was thankful. We told him we'd pray for him and headed back to rejoin Joy and the men.

As we walked away, I was thinking the most important part of this little ministry experience was sharing my testimony with the man. But I soon learned differently as Sarah reflected on our encounter. "You know, Mom, I've heard you and Dad talk a lot about the people you've witnessed to, but it was so neat for me to watch you actually do it. I've never seen that before." I realized that the ministry in the park that day was also in the life of my 13 year-old daughter who now had a real-life example in her mind of what it means to witness to someone. I've explained to her how to witness, and I've shared my witnessing "war stories" with her, but I had never modeled a personal witness for her in real life. God turned a simple witnessing encounter into a ministry training time with one of my children.

Jesus was constantly teaching by example for his disciples, modeling to them what he wanted them to learn. He healed the multitudes and held a child, fed the thousands and encouraged a friend, taught the crowds and touched the lonely. His disciples were always with him as he ministered love to men and women, children and elders, families and friendless, wealthy and outcasts, lovely and lepers. They watched as he displayed his power, expressed his anger, showed his sorrow, and served in humility. They listened as he taught his truth to the simple, the wise, the learned, and the uneducated. When he looked on the multitudes with compassion, and prayed for more workers for the harvest, his disciples saw him day after day modeling the life of a compassionate worker in God's harvest fields. Though his disciples were slow to understand his teachings, they could not deny the powerful, living model of ministry he presented to them. Whatever words they remembered, they would never forget the life they witnessed.

Discipleship of your children is at best anemic without a living example of what a follower of Christ looks like, acts like, thinks, says, and does. I cannot overstate it enough that one of your highest priorities in discipling your children should be that they will imitate your life (Phil. 4:9). Of course, that raises the bar pretty high. If I want my children someday to be mature Christian adults, then I must be committed now to giving them a living example of what a mature Christian adult looks like.

Even today, as I work on the final chapters of this book, this principle of discipleship was laid in my lap. We came down to Walnut Springs so the children could play and visit with their grandmother while Clay and I locked ourselves away in our rooms to work. The deadline is upon us, so I told my children to consider me invisible. I guess invisibility isn't one of my better traits because three times in the last two hours I have had to leave the seclusion of my room to referee fusses. Rather than doing it with a frustrated attitude, though, I maintained a mature, self-controlled attitude. That living example of maturity, I like to think, had an influence on the result of my intervention. My oldest child shared a verse with the other children, confessed that she had acted selfishly, and asked forgiveness. My younger child involved in the contention hugged the oldest and said, "It's not your fault. I'm sorry. You want a cookie?" And then to me he said, "Mommy, how did you manage to make all of us feel better?"

Being a living example takes time and effort. But it makes a difference. If you have a heart for discipling your children, there is perhaps no more powerful tool for turning your child into a disciple of Jesus than through the power of a living example of Christianity.

❧

Discipleship is a life, it's not a lesson. And I can think of no better example of these qualities being lived out in a family, and their impact on the life of a child, than in my own life growing up in the Bone home with John and Wanda. I'm quite certain that my mother probably never used or even thought of the term "discipleship" to describe what happened in our home, but it was every bit the discipleship environment that I believe God intended the home and family to be. I know because all three of her children love the Lord and are serving him today.

When it came to personal relationship, my mother excelled. She was a warm, vibrant, real person all of the time. There was always an open channel between our hearts, even during my adolescent years. She would talk to me about everything, and I felt like I could talk to her about anything. She would comfort me when I was sad, laugh with me when I was happy, pick me up when I stumbled, and even support my causes. Instead of building her career, she chose to stay home and build relationships.

As to spiritual intent and living example, my parents always just talked about the Lord at home and lived by biblical principles. There was no clever Christian curriculum or popular author or outline that did it for them. They just lived it. They taught us about stewardship, and demonstrated it through generous giving and living. They taught us about marriage, and showed us what loyalty, devotion, and commitment looked like. They taught us about integrity, and lived honestly and morally 24 hours each day. Mom shared her favorite Bible verses with us, Dad always prayed, we always went to church, and they showed us together how to trust God in trials. They were consistent not just at home, but in all their varied interests and activities, from golfing and gardening, to the country club and the corporate world. They simply lived what they believed.

When I got to college, others took up where my parents left off, but they built on the foundation already laid by my parents at home. There was already a heart for God beating within me because of my dear mother's commitment to loving, personal relationship with her only daughter, her spiritual intent in passing along the life of faith to me, and her living example of godly motherhood. She made me hungry for the things of God, and able to receive all he had to give. After 25 years of ministry as an adult, I can honestly say it all started at home, in the heart of my mother, and in her faithful testimony for the Lord.

That is an encouragement to me as a mother, as I now try to relate personally to my own children, carry out my spiritual intentions in their lives, and try to give them a living example of Christianity. I probably will never make it through a study of the entire Bible with my children, or even study a tenth of the topics that I hope to with them. I'm sure they won't know all the definitions and related scriptures of the top twenty character qualities of a mature Christian. And they won't memorize all the wonderful scriptures that I had hoped they would. But they'll be ready to be followers of Christ. They'll be his disciples.

è

If I accomplish nothing else in filling in the blanks on the biblical outline of discipleship, though, let it be that these three qualities stand out in bold letters—that my children knew my heart for them from my personal relationship with them; that they knew my heart for truth from the spiritual intent that I had for each of them; and, that they knew my heart for God from the living example I lived before them.

One of the simplest but clearest descriptions of discipleship in the gospels is Mark 3:14a: "He appointed twelve—designating them apostles—that they might be with him..." The disciples, also called apostles ("sent ones") were to be "with him," with Jesus. If you boiled it down to the barest outline of discipleship, that is it. To be "with him." If I want my children to become disciples of Jesus, I can't think of a more "with him" place for that to happen than in my home. As Jesus lives in and through Clay and me, and my children live 24 hours a day around us, they are "with him" through us. As we bring the life of Christ into the everyday routines of our home and family life, my children are "with him." As they see us navigate the triumphs and trials of life as Christian parents, they are "with him."

Joy became a "follower" of the *The Promise* just from being with us. We didn't try hard to make her that way, or constantly grill her and drill her on why she should be a follower and on everything she needed to know. We simply loved her and loved what we were doing. Joy will always be a picture to me of what discipleship should be if everything else is stripped away. I believe my children will become followers of Jesus Christ in much the same way.

God never intended discipleship of children to be difficult, or complicated, or burdensome, or a matter for the "experts." I think he meant it to be as simple as a loving personal relationship, guided and infused with spiritual intent, fleshed out through a living example.

❦

Thoughts On the Living Word

We're all pretty clear when it comes to the message of salvation. Most of us can quote John 3:16 in our sleep. But when it comes to talking about discipleship, and what should happen after we're saved, the view gets pretty clouded. Too often, the path to growth in Christ sounds more like a cold, technical procedure than the warm relationship with Christ that led to our step of salvation. But a careful look at Scripture will clear the air about discipleship. It really is just a continuation of the relationship with Christ that was begun at salvation, only growing deeper and stronger as we grow closer. When we "make disciples" of our children, we are simply letting them follow along and join in the living, learning, and loving relationship we have with our Savior.

Matthew 28:18-20

Jesus had one command for the apostles as he turned over his ministry to them—"make disciples (followers)." How did Jesus say they were to make followers of him? How would "baptizing" someone make them a follower of Christ? What kinds of things were they to teach those who became followers? How do you know Jesus is "with you always" in that process? How does all this apply to you as a parent?

John 13:3-7

On the night he was to die, Jesus greeted the twelve disciples with an important lesson. What was Jesus teaching by his example? Why couldn't he just tell them what they needed to know? What impact do you think his actions would have on his disciples? Are there any living examples that your young disciples need to see? What?

Philippians 4:9

Paul encouraged the faithful Philippians to live godly lives. What was Paul saying about his own life? How do you see personal relationship, spiritual intent and living example in his words? Are you able to say these words, without reservation, to your children? What would they "put into practice" if they imitated your life and teaching?

2 Timothy 2:1,2

Paul instructs his pastoral protégé, Timothy, that it is not enough only to know about Christ, but that he needed to pass that knowledge on to others. What does it mean to be "strong in the grace that is in Jesus Christ"? What kind of spiritual intent did Paul exhort Timothy to have? How does this verse relate to you as a Christian parent?

My Thoughts

_____

_____

_____

_____

_____

_____

_____

_____

_____

_____

_____

_____

Thoughts On Living the Word

Clay and I both try to take each of our children out alone periodically so we can spend time with them one-on-one. I use it as a time to gently probe their thoughts, feelings, fears, and dreams, and to share my own heart as well. No matter which child it is, they never fail to respond or to open their hearts when I make time for them. ❧ If I teach a class at church, I try to have Sarah with me as a helper, even if it means she would miss her own age-group class. She never complains, though, because we have such a good time. I get to be a living example of teaching the word. ❧ We talk quite a bit about ministry in our family, but until the kids actually have something to do, their spirits aren't really engaged with the words. I need to be just as intentional about making ministry happen as a regular part of our lives as I am about making education happen. Whether it's a "plate of cookies" outreach in the neighborhood, visiting at the nursing home, or a short-term mission trip to Mexico, I've got to give them the opportunity to serve.

My Life

Personal application: Read John 13:3-7 in your quiet time this week. As you meditate on the example Christ left to us, consider specific ways that you can "wash your children's feet" this week. Simply serve them as Jesus would and observe their reactions and responses.

Family application: Make a time with each of your children over the next few weeks to take them to the "dinner of their dreams." Use the time with them to probe their dreams of how God might use them someday, or what they want to become. Record them for posterity.

Winter ~ Season *of* Reflection

Winter
Thoughts on Reflection
Ten Years Later

After driving fifteen hours through the desolate, snow-covered plains of Missouri and Kansas along Interstate 70, we were all quite relieved to be able to untangle our restless legs for a brief stop. Colby, Kansas is a veritable oasis of food and drink on this otherwise mostly unpopulated stretch of highway. A steaming cup of hot chocolate and a quick meal would give us the fuel we needed for the last leg of our journey back home.

Sarah, Joel, Joy, and I had just completed a five-day, 2,300-mile trip to Kentucky and Tennessee, and back to Colorado. Every part of our travel-weary bodies longed for the warmth of home, and for our own inviting beds to snuggle up in on this frigid winter's evening. We all piled back into the car for what should be an easy, two-hour, 200-mile sprint home.

What the weather channel said would be "light" snow, though, turned heavier as we left the Interstate for the last sixty miles. As we neared our home near the foothills of the Rockies, high winds blowing the heavy snow created a white-out that left us sometimes crawling along at a snail's pace. Joel gripped the steering wheel tightly, leaning forward to see the disappearing road, just trying not slip into the snow drifts on the side of the road.

Joy whispered a prayer for us in the back seat, which we all agreed with silently in our hearts. At only 12 years old, she did not remember being on such a snowy adventure, and was understandably a little frightened. However, experience from numerous such trips brought some peace to my own heart. I could still remember when, as newly-weds, Clay and I had to inch our way from New Mexico, where we had visited my parents for Christmas, toward our Colorado home. An unexpected blizzard blanketed the land and roads with deep snow, which made our drive home frightening for me as a young woman. Then there were the journeys to Texas when we would get caught in the grip of terrifying storms driving over high passes. Yet, God had always faithfully brought us to safety, so I sat in the backseat with Joy, massaging her hands and trying to distract her from her anxieties.

Sarah, sensing Joy's mood, told her about her trip with Joel just one year before coming back from Seattle. "We were traveling on a road of black ice. Twenty cars slipped to the side of the road right in front of us. It was like a dream, Joy! But we went slowly, ever-onward with home in our minds, and we made it through the worst roads I ever remembered. So don't you worry, you are in good hands with Joel. He is a seasoned storm driver and he will get us through! Let's turn on some Christmas music and look at the sparkling beauty as we drive!"

Finally, after five-and-a-half hours, we reached our neighborhood, and exhaled oversized sighs of relief as we turned into our driveway. It was late, but Clay and Nathan had lighted the house, turned on the Christmas tree lights, and opened the garage door to welcome us home! A singing tea kettle and a blazing fireplace told us that we were indeed safely home.

&

Our trip, squeezed into the last days before Christmas, seemed essential as we visited one of my oldest friends, Gwen, who had become a sort of sister I had never had. She had made the effort to travel for 26 years to see our family and to bring suitcases full of presents for each of us during the Christmas season. This year, though, she would not make it as the care of her 94 year-old mother meant she could not leave home.

Another event, though, also drew us to the southeast. Seventeen years before, when we were living in Nashville, the Lord had led Clay and me to start a homeschool support group. We left two years later, but the group continued, and would eventually be named Whole Heart Academy, in honor of our ministry. My dear friends, who had started the group with me, were hosting their annual Christmas luncheon. Lisa Hamilton, Marla Huskey, and Jennie Monroe had led the group for all these years. Lynn Custer, my dear friend and a Whole Heart Ministries board member, was flying in from North Carolina. We all started the group because we believed that homeschooling mothers need spiritual support, accountability, and encouragement to stay committed to their ideals on this journey of faith.

These godly women had weathered many life-storms, fears, and bouts of weariness, and yet they kept moving forward, and had faithfully traveled the long road of homeschooling. We had started out together when our children were quite young, and now we had all lived through seasons of babies, childhood schooling, teenaged hormones and independence, and young adult launchings from our homes. We were veteran travelers.

How delightful to spend my last evening with these sweet friends, sipping our coffee and tea together, and reflecting on lessons we had learned. We all started out with typically unseasoned high ideals and over-reaching plans for parenting and homeschooling. Yet now, having been "seasoned" by nearly twenty years of experience, all agreed that prayer had become a top priority for our children. We all knew that we were not in control of our lives or our children's lives, but that by God's grace, we and they would make it. We would look to God, now, for the fruit.

"Remember how we all fretted and worried about which classes our children needed, and what was the best curriculum?" one of my friends commented. "We compared our kids to everyone else's children and spent so much extra, wasted time on worrying about things that didn't count," .

"So then," I asked, "what are you telling all of these young moms now who are so deeply entrenched in homeschooling?" Each of my old friends spiritedly agreed that the training of children in excellent moral character, building patterns of greatness into their hearts, and giving foundations of truth and faith, were all so much more important than anything else.

"The one thing I wish I had done so much more," one my friends shared, "was to have spent much more personal time with each child. I let the duties of housework and life crowd out the heart time. I really think I could have had a more profound impact on my children if I had chosen to invest more of my time with them."

Our conversation reinforced for me just how important personal, heartfelt mentoring was and is in the life of my own children. I have the opportunity every day to teach them wisdom, encourage godly character, model unconditional love, affirm gifts and convictions, and exhort them to excellence. Jesus used only the power of personal relationship to prepare his disciples to serve him and change the world. He gave them his time, love, touch, teaching, and life—he imprinted his life on their hearts, and it changed their lives forever. They were "with him," and in the same way, my children are with me. And that is the true power of homeschooling.

Even so, I have known too many moms who, out of discouragement, fear, or tiredness, decided simply to quit homeschooling their children, or even worse, to quit their marriages or their faith. Winter seasons of motherhood can be difficult, so we need to be prepared to stand strong in faith. That is not to deny the reality of depressing seasons, or to underestimate the difficulties of living in a fallen world. I have faced very real times of darkness and temptation to despair, yet with God's help I determined in my heart not become a victim of my circumstances, or to give into bitterness, depression, or discouragement. Instead, I have learned to "take joy" even in my winter seasons, and let God give life and light to my heart.

The distance between despair and hope can be but a hair's breadth, a slight turning of the heart away from one and toward the other. If I turn away from God to despair, I create a chasm that can swallow up everything good God has for me. But if I turn toward God, by faith, he'll begin to fill the empty places in my heart with his hope and goodness. When I honestly face my own dark thoughts, and choose God instead, that changes me, and makes me a stronger, more loving woman with a greater love for God.

How I respond in my winter seasons of motherhood also affects my children. If I resist dark feelings, and choose instead to turn to God, I plant a flag of confidence in his goodness and in his promises, and my children can see that. Often, I could see in their eyes that they wanted me to be okay—to choose joy. So, many times, in the quiet glow of candlelight in my bedroom, behind closed doors, I would give my burden of darkness to the Lord.

I have spoken to thousands of women over the years. Like me, they are dealing with the stresses, fears, and anxieties of life, pouring out their lives daily for their families. Most women I know, including my dearest friends, carry a potentially life-darkening burden of some kind. They give me another reason to be faithful and to trust God, so I can be a source of hope to other mothers. His faithfulness and goodness is the foundation for every story I tell. It is real to me because I have experienced it.

ª

As I have reflected on the winter seasons of my life as a mother, I can see that, though they could be very trying times, they also have been times when I learned the deepest lessons of faith, and when I grew closer to God. Let me share with you some of the fruit of my own winter reflections.

First, I have learned that *my life is not the center of the universe.* Despite how I may feel, when hard times invade my life, I know that God doesn't "have it out" for me. It has taken me years to see just how self-centered and selfish I can be, and just how much growing up I needed to do. Jesus said that in this world, we would have tribulation, so struggle is a normal part of life. He certainly had it, and so did Peter, Paul, David, Moses, Esther, and all who have lived for the purposes of God. My struggles are not exceptions needing special attention; they are simply the norm.

Second, I have learned that *motherhood, and the raising of godly children, invites intense spiritual warfare.* You probably didn't think about that when you came to Christ, but you can't ignore it the longer and more deeply you come to know him. Living as a Christian is not just about believing in Jesus, enjoying God's blessings, and then going to heaven.

That kind of mediocrity of soul is never an option for a mature believer. God says the Christian life is spiritual warfare, a battle, and we all will have to fight. No exceptions. Paul said, "do not be surprised at the fiery ordeal among you, which comes upon you for your testing, as though some strange thing were happening to you" (1 Pet. 4:12, NASB). It's just normal life.

Third, I have learned that *God is transcendent, with infinite purposes beyond my finite comprehension.* God is God, and I am not! He has been faithful to each generation of his people, compassionate and merciful even when we cannot see or understand his purposes. That truth forces a choice in my heart: either I bow my knee to God's will, trusting his grace to sustain me through every struggle because I know he is sovereign and in control; or, I give in to my bitterness, allowing grief and despair to defeat me. It is a choice I have to make over and over again. God allowed Satan to test Job. When Job asked God to explain the reason for his suffering, God did not explain to him what he had done, but rather reminded Job who he was—the Creator of the universe and all creation. In the end, Job realized that the answer to his question was not in knowing *why* he suffered, but in knowing *who* he worshiped. He submitted to God's sovereignty and purpose.

Fourth, I have learned that *God wants to shape me, his child, into the likeness of Christ.* Scripture teaches that "God disciplines us for our good, that we may share in his holiness" (Heb. 12:10). His hand of discipline has loosed my grip on things I hold too tightly—possessions, people, dreams, pride, expectations—things I have placed my hope in instead of in him. In their place, he has given me the wonderful freedom of knowing I am loved and accepted by him, no matter how I may sin or fail him. I have confidence and hope in him because of his grace and mercy, his compassion that covers all my hurts and wounds, his justice that will right the wrongs I have known, and his love that catches all my tears. When I let go of things in this life, into my open hands God places Jesus, who is enough.

Fifth, I have learned that *God uses my trials to make me better able to minister to other women.* I have learned compassion for others who struggle, because I have grappled with my own issues. I have wrestled with children, marriage, finances, health, and so many other issues, so I can more easily identify with others in similar situations, and offer them the compassion and hope that I have found in God's faithfulness and goodness. God "comforts us in all our troubles, so that we can comfort those in any trouble with the comfort we ourselves have received from God" (2 Cor. 1:3-4).

Finally, I have learned that *God uses hard times to make me stronger and more faithful*. I have a much larger capacity now, than I ever had as a young woman, to handle challenges and responsibilities. A young mom might be overwhelmed with the constant work and stress of having a new baby, but a mom who has many children learns to take her many responsibilities in stride. The capacity to handle more has been trained into her life by the gradual increase of responsibility. It may take some time, but I really can "consider it all joy" when I "face trials of many kinds," because I know the "testing of [my] faith develops perseverance" (Jas. 1:1-2).

ಜ

So, winter is a season for reflection. For all the darkness I may associate with winter, I have discovered that the winter seasons of my life can also be times of peace, reflection, and even quiet rest, if I will let them be. A winter season can force me to slow down, reflect on life, wait on God, and trust him. It can seem that everything is dead in winter, that nothing is happening, but that is never true. Under the surface of the winter snows there is always the continuation of life—roots really are growing deeper, sap is being stored, energy is being conserved. Winter is not an end, but a transition. The abundant and unstoppable life of spring is about to break forth out of winter, and a new beginning is coming.

In the same way, my roots are growing deeper in the winter seasons of motherhood, the Holy Spirit is within me, and my energy is being conserved, all with one goal in view—that there will be new life and new fruit coming from me. Winter is a time to diligently and faithfully store up his word in my spirit, drink deeply of his goodness and mercy, and keep the fires of hope alive in my heart. It is a time to stop, and reflect on how my life is different because I am God's child, and on what is really most important in my life with him—my husband, my children, my family, my friends. It is a time to look for signs of life.

Winter is a good time to reflect on Romans 8:28, to see how "in all things God works for the good of those who love him, who have been called according to his purpose." It is a good time to reflect on Jesus' encouragement, that "I have told you these things, so that in me you may have peace. In this world you will have trouble. But take heart! I have overcome the world" (Jn. 16:33). It is a good time to recall, with Jeremiah, that "Because of the Lord's great love we are not consumed, for his compassions never fail. They are new every morning; great is your faithfulness. I say to myself, 'The Lord is my portion; therefore I will wait for him.' The Lord is good to those who hope is in him, to the one who seeks him" (Lam. 3:22-25). Winter is a good time to reflect on what you know is true.

On the final leg of our long journey to the southeast and back to Colorado, we passed through a winter season. Everything was gray, it was difficult, and we were tired. But even when we could not see the road beneath the snow, still we kept our hearts focused on the hope of home. Even when we saw other cars abandoned in the snow drifts, still we knew our safe, warm home was waiting. And when we finally made it home, we reflected on God's faithfulness and goodness to us. Motherhood is a long journey along an uncertain road of life, but "take heart," God is with you. He will never leave you or forsake you. He's with you all the way home.

May God grant you the courage to "take heart" in the midst of your winter seasons, to reflect on what you know is true, to wait on him, and to hope in the power of the resurrection promised in the season ahead. May he quiet your spirit with his peace as you reflect upon the winter landscape of your life, and anticipate the promise of new life in the coming of spring.

❦

Winter

*Therefore, since we have a great high priest
who has gone through the heavens, Jesus the
Son of God, let us hold firmly to the faith we
profess.*

*For we do not have a high priest who is unable
to sympathize with our weaknesses, but we
have one who has been tempted in every way,
just as we are—yet was without sin.*

*Let us then approach the throne of grace with
confidence, so that we may receive mercy and
find grace to help us in our time of need.*

Hebrews 4:14-16

"We pray for our children because we must pray. We are desperately needy people living in a broken world, and we have the privilege, through prayer, to connect with the Almighty, to see God intervene in our children's lives and in our own lives. God is our only hope."

William & Nancie Carmichael
Lord Bless My Child

Chapter Ten

Prayers from Home

*Let us then approach the throne of grace with
confidence, so that we may receive mercy and
find grace to help us in our time of need.*

Finally, it was quiet. The kids were in bed, the baby was asleep, and I was alone. Alone! It had been a very long and busy day, full of housework, schoolwork, a new baby, long car trips, and the constant needs of a household of children and adults. But it was over, and now I was ready to have a well-deserved evening of rest just to myself. As I slumped onto the den couch, I exhaled a deep and weary sigh that came from way down deep inside of me. It was met by a familiar voice.

"Mama?" (I can always tell when Sarah needs to talk when she calls me "Mama"). I looked around to see my 12 year-old "little" girl peeking through the doorway, her sweet almost-young-woman face and teary eyes saying, "Please, may I talk to you for just a moment? It really is important." I took a deep spiritual breath, reached down into my weary heart, and found a tiny bit of energy left that I didn't know was there.

"Come on in honey. What's wrong?" I had grown accustomed to these late-night, soul-searching, heart-revealing talks with Sarah. When Clay is gone or working late, and the boys are in bed, she will often stay up later just to talk about what's on her mind, sometimes serious and sometimes silly. This night, it was serious.

Over the next several minutes, she poured out her heart about something that she had struggled with for two years, a problem she just could not resolve. It wasn't the problem that caught my heart, though, it was something else she said as she finished her thoughts. "You know, Mom, sometimes I wonder if God is really real. My prayers seem to stop at the ceiling. I feel like I'm just saying words to myself. How do you know that what you and Daddy have taught us is really true? How can you be sure you're not just believing in a nice story?"

That's when I felt a sense of panic strike at my heart. Sarah had loved Jesus since she was a young child, and was unusually tender-hearted toward God for her age, so I knew this was a serious question. But in addition to my concern for Sarah, I found that her questions caused me to start questioning myself! Had I failed somehow to strengthen her faith? Was there something I missed in her spiritual training? Were these the seeds of unbelief that would lead her away from God?

As I shook off those disturbing thoughts, I suggested that we pray. The prayer of my heart was definitely more for me than for her, even though the words on my lips were for her. Then we talked. My words of counsel to her were sufficient for the moment, assuring her that her doubts were not unusual, that God is big enough to work through them with her, and that her father and I were here to help her. We prayed and she went to bed reassured. I went to bed disturbed.

In my time of prayer the next morning, I had to admit to the Lord that I was deeply concerned for my precious daughter. The panic I had felt the night before had become a gnawing fear. What if, after all my efforts, my children do not have a heart for God? What if I don't do enough to put them on the path of a godly life? What if they join the growing list of teenaged children we know, raised in homeschooling families, who have rebelled against God, or simply rejected Christianity?

I agonized over these questions for a while as I conversed with God. But I began to notice that the more I prayed, the more the fear ebbed. The more time I spent with the Father, the more at peace I became. And then it hit me—I was simply following my own best advice to Sarah the night before. God was reassuring me that my doubts and concerns were not that unusual, and that he was big enough to work through them with me.

By the time I said, "Amen," my heart was at peace. I had met with the Father, entrusted my children's lives into his hands, and been renewed in my spirit to remain faithful to my calling as a Christian mother. But I came away with much more than just temporary spiritual relief. I came away with a clearer understanding of how prayer fits into the picture of parenting.

When I pray for my children, it really isn't just for them—after all, God is in control of their lives. It is really just as much for me. God, the heavenly Father, wants me to talk with him, and to become a part of what he is doing in the lives of my children. More than all the things I do to turn my children to God, my prayer time is the most important part of my homeschooling day because it is what turns me to God.

Seeing God's hand of providence

When I am praying to God, I am forced to acknowledge his providence and control over every detail of my life. I quickly see that I certainly am not in control, but he is. I acknowledge before him my inadequacy to meet my children's needs, and my inability to be the kind of mother I really want to be, but I can trust God to finish the work he has begun in my children's lives. I confess my struggles and negative attitudes, and cry to him that I can't seem to overcome them, but I ask for God's mercy and strength to grow as a parent. I cannot train every area of my children's character, or instill every value I know they will need, but I can ask for God's hand of providence to guide them in the way of righteousness in spite of my shortcomings. God is sovereign whether or not I pray to him, but I do not really see his hand of providence in my life until I turn the eyes of my heart to him in prayer.

David knew that God was sovereign. "All the days ordained for me were written in your book before one of them came to be" (Ps. 139:16). In the beautiful prayer of Psalm 139, David's spirit finds rest in the knowledge that God's hand providentially leads him, no matter where he may be or what may happen to him. For me, the greatest benefit of prayer is that it forces me to acknowledge, like David did, that "God is there." Prayer opens my heart to his reality and puts all the earthly details of my life into heavenly perspective. And if "God is there" for me, then that will be true for my children, too.

Yet all too often, I act as though that is not true. I begin to believe that I alone am responsible for how my children turn out. I wrongly think that because I am committed to training my children in righteousness, and to homeschooling them, and to doing all the "right" things for them, that somehow that is a guarantee that they will turn out alright. I am like the soldier who would depend on his chariot or his sword for victory in battle, when in truth "the battle belongs to the Lord."

It is so easy to fall into the trap of trusting in methods rather than trusting in God. We wouldn't admit to it, but we often think and act like Christian behaviorists who believe that we are responsible for what our children become. If we do the right kind of character training, they'll have character; if we fail to, they'll have character flaws. If they memorize enough Scripture, they'll be spiritual; if they don't, they'll be at risk. We lose sight of the sovereign God who shepherds our children, and we focus narrowly on what we are or are not doing, worrying unnecessarily and vainly, "It's all up to me!" We inadvertently begin to think we are just as important as God in our children's lives.

At the end of the day (or at the end of the homeschooling!), the fate of my children will not be determined by whether I've used the right materials, read the best books, taken enough field trips, or done more of whatever I didn't do enough of. God is in control of their lives, not I. How they turn out might depend more on how much I prayed for them, more on how much

I depended on God for them, rather than on how much I did for them. I want to be able to say to my child that I am "confident of this, that he who began a good work in you will carry it on to completion until the day of Christ Jesus" (Phil. 1:6).

Approaching the throne of grace

The older I grow, the more I realize how dependent I am upon God's grace. Without a steady flow of his grace into my life every day, I am sure I would degenerate into some kind of tyrant-mother, barking orders at my children with a zero-tolerance standard of behavior. Life is simply too demanding to try to do it all without God's grace—washing, cleaning, cooking, schooling, training, taking, fixing, talking, ad infinitum. If I am to be the mother God wants me to be for my children, I cannot do it without God's grace.

Grace is a rather abstract concept, I know, but there are times in Scripture that it seems quite concrete—God has it, we need it, we ask, God gives. We can go to the "throne of grace with confidence" where we will "find grace to help us in our time of need" (Heb. 4:16). Scripture describes it almost as a tangible resource that we must acquire for godly living. In many ways, it is the spiritual equivalent of physical sustenance for our bodies. We cannot survive physically without food, and we cannot survive spiritually without grace.

The writer of Hebrews said, "Let us then approach the throne of grace with confidence, so that we may receive mercy and find grace to help us in our time of need." When I feel the weight of parenting pressing down on me unrelentingly, mercy is appreciated—I need to know there is a merciful God who knows and cares about me. Grace is more than just appreciated, though, it is necessary—I need spiritual strength to carry the burden of parenting and keep going. And that is what I receive when I come to God's throne of grace in prayer. Prayer is a "means of grace" by which God releases more of his grace into my life. Without prayer, I cut off a major source of the grace of God.

We were all at an AWANA awards night meeting recently (it's a church -based Bible club). While I was at the back with Joy, I began to notice the families throughout the room. For nearly two hours, small children were in and out of their parents' laps, wiggling in their seats, whimpering, smiling, talking and doing all kinds of antics while the parents sat patiently waiting for their children to receive their awards. It was somehow a small picture for me of what goes on in all their homes all day long—the constant, ongoing demands of being a godly parent trying to raise up a godly heritage. And it is only the grace of God working in their lives that keeps them going day-in and day-out.

As we drove back home that night, I looked at my own children. They were all a-twitter about the awards they had received, or about what tasty foods they ate from the potluck supper, or how much fun they had with their friends playing outside. They were so innocent and carefree, just enjoying life as God meant children to do. I thought to myself that they had no concept of the real burdens and struggles of life. They could not conceive what it feels like to be a parent, carrying the responsibility for young lives. But it was as though God said to me, "That's why I made you a parent. So, by my grace, you can let them be children." That's why I, and all those other parents, need God's grace every day—so we can give our children the gift of childhood. I approach God's throne so he can give me all the grace I need to give my children all the life they need.

Standing firm in God's Spirit

If life were free of temptation, I would have no need to trust God with my children. If life were easy, I would have no need of God's grace. But the plain reality is that life is dangerous and difficult, and we cannot live it without God.

Unless you have sequestered yourself and your children in a remote mountain cabin with no contact with the outside world, you do not need to be convinced that "our struggle is not against flesh and blood, but against the rulers, against the authorities, against the powers of this dark world and against the spiritual forces of evil in the heavenly realms" (Eph. 6:12, NASB). Evil and wickedness permeates every pore of our culture. But praise be to God that the battle belongs to the Lord!

The doubts that Sarah was having were not just of her own making, just as my own doubts the next morning were not. Satan has been sowing seeds of doubt in God's people since the beginning of creation. His temporary "victory" over Eve, and then Adam, has created the battleground where he now wages his fiercest attacks—in the hearts and minds of humankind. For those who follow God, Satan's weapons strike deep in the inner parts of our being—fear, doubt, uncertainty, despair, lust, deceit, pride. Sarah's and my little struggles were just a small example of the kinds of battles that take place in the spiritual realm for hearts and minds.

As a parent, I am constantly aware of my need to be armed for this battle. I cannot ignore the picture of the Christian in Ephesians 6:10-18 who is outfitted with the "full armor of God." I notice several significant things about that Christian. First, he has only one defensive weapon—"take up the *shield of faith*, with which you can extinguish all the flaming arrows of the evil one." His faith in God is his best defense against Satan's lies. Second, he has only one offensive weapon—"Take...the *sword of the Spirit*, which is the word of God." He fights back against Satan's attacks with the double-edged sword of God's truth. And, third, he has only one strategic command to obey—"And *pray in the Spirit* on all occasions with all kinds of prayers and requests. With this in mind, be alert and always keep on praying for all the saints." His offensive strategy is to pray for God's help and intervention, not just for himself but for all believers.

Concerning that prayer, though, it easy to overlook a critical truth. It is not just the act of praying, or the words of prayer that are in view. It is the source of the prayer. Only prayer that is "in the Spirit" will have the power to defeat the enemy against whom I pray. It is only as my life is yielded to the Holy Spirit that I will have any kind of victory over Satan's onslaughts. If I am praying in my "flesh," I will have no power to defeat Satan. He is more powerful than my sinful flesh. But "greater is He who is in [me] than he who is in the world" (1 Jn. 4:4, NASB). If I am letting God's Spirit live through me, by confessing my sin and appropriating his strength, then the power of Christ's resurrection will flow through me and my prayers. And when that power is aimed at Satan, there is only one Victor.

As a parent of some of those "saints" that I am called to pray for in the Spirit, I cannot take lightly my role in godly warfare. My children need me to pray for them as they engage in their own spiritual battles. I will not always be able to be with them as they grow, but I can always pray for them...for God's providence and grace as they find their own places in his plan, and as they learn to trust their Heavenly Father with their lives.

Praising the Lord

"Praise to the Lord, to God our Savior, who daily bears our burdens." Perhaps this is the prayer my children need most from me. The prayer of praise to God. When my lips are opened in praise to God for who he is and what he has done, I cannot help but think that heaven opens upon our family. I can envision in my mind the light of God's presence glowing in and around our humble little home. I might even hear an angel choir singing the "Amen!" to my praise. It reminds me of the words to a popular song, "Praise the Lord! He can work through those who praise him. Praise the Lord! For our God inhabits praise." (Ps. 22:2 KJV) When I turn my heart in praise to my Creator, he inhabits my home.

Unfortunately, it is all too easy to inadvertently trivialize prayer. Without praise, my prayers can become little more than a special request line to a heavenly Daddy who says "no" only if I don't ask nicely enough. Of course, that is immature prayer. It is the spiritual equivalent of an immature child who comes to his father only to ask for privileges and toys, never expressing his love, admiration, or respect for that father. I suppose we can all find that kind of immaturity in our prayers at one time or another. I know I can. But I also know I am discovering as I grow and mature what kind of prayer God desires, and it begins with a heart of praise, not petition.

Early in my Christian life I learned an acronym for prayer that has stayed with me—ACTS. Its letters stand for Adoration, Confession, Thanksgiving, and Supplication. Admittedly, it is an oversimplified memory device, but it reflects the priority of praise and adoration in our prayers. God wants our praise first. When I truly understand how great and majestic my Creator God is, and how utterly dependent upon him I am for life, much less the things of life, then what else can I do but offer praise to him? I don't deserve to ask anything of him if I cannot praise him first. There is no depth to praiseless prayer.

God, deliver me from shallow prayer that tells my children, not that you are here with us, but that you are "up there" somewhere, listening from the distance, only involved when you have to be. God of the universe, let my children hear your praise coming from my lips and heart. Let them know your presence and reality, that you are not "out there" but "right here." That is what I want most for my children. I want them to know and experience the reality and the presence of the God who made them. If all they hear from me is pious prayers and petty petitions, they will miss you. Let them find you in my praise for you.

❧

Most of my work as a homeschooling mother can be finished—it has a definite beginning and a point of completion that allows me to say, "That's done, what's next." But prayer, the most important work I can do for my children, is not like that—it is never really finished. I can finish a lesson, complete a unit, discipline my children, and organize my house, and all those tasks are done. But the work of prayer is never "done." If anything, the work expands as the children grow, and more prayer is needed every passing year.

Unlike homeschooling goals, though, prayer is not a task to be accomplished and checked off a list. Prayer is a relationship to be enjoyed. My responsibility is simply to cultivate my relationship with God who wants to meet with me and hear from me. God wants me to come to him, just like

Sarah came to me. He is my Heavenly Father, and I am his child. He longs and loves for me simply to come and share my heart with him. Not just when I have troubles and needs, but all the time. That's what fathers and children do—they talk. It isn't a task or a chore to pray, it is a wonderful relationship with my loving Father. It is being close to him because I admire him, and respect him, and want to learn from him.

The more time I spend with my Father in prayer, the better prepared I will be to help my children. And even more important, the more I can rest in the Lord knowing, by faith, that my children are in his hands. When I can trust in God's providence, draw upon his grace, join in the spiritual battle through prayer, and praise his name, all the other things I do as a mother seem to pale in significance. The more I grow as a mother, the more I grow convinced that the most important impact I will ever have on my children will be through my prayers for them.

Sometimes I feel like I have fallen to my knees out of exhaustion, tiredness, or frustration. But no matter what has brought me to my knees, that is right where God wants me. It is only from being on my knees in prayer that I will have the strength and assurance to stand up and keep going as a mother. The battle belongs to the Lord. Amen!

❦

Thoughts On the Living Word

Our focus in prayer is too often on the prayer itself—what we want God to do or to provide. God's focus in prayer, though, is always on the pray-er, the one praying—what does that person really need from him. Even more than changing our circumstances, God knows that prayer changes us, and that is what he is most interested in. When we pray to God, we become active participants in the unfolding drama of what he is already doing in our lives. The main thing he wants is what we really need—to trust in his sovereignty and love as he works out his will in our lives. That trust, though, comes only from spending time with him, and wanting to be intimately involved in what he is doing. That is the essence of prayer—fellowship with God, our Father.

Matthew 6:5-15

Jesus teaches his followers what prayer is not, and what it should be. What makes prayer "hypocritical"? What kind of prayer does God "reward"? Do you ever "babble" on with whatever requests or thoughts come into your mind? Does your prayer sound like a conversation or an announcement? If God already knows your needs, how should that affect how you pray to him? If you used the Lord's prayer as a pattern, how would you pray?

Matthew 7:7-12

Jesus teaches his followers to pray purposefully and confidently. What might you "ask" for in prayer? "seek"? "knock"? Do you always "receive"? "find"? "open"? How might God answer these prayers differently than you expect? If God answers differently, do you have any reason to fear his response? Why, or why not?

Hebrews 4:14-16

The writer tells his Jewish Christian readers that they have confident access directly to the Father through faith. When you pray for your children, how confident do you feel about your prayers? Are you confident that you will "receive mercy" and "find grace" when you go to the throne God in prayer? What is the source of your confidence?

Hebrews 10:19-22

The writer goes on to encourage them to "draw near to God." How do you know when your heart is sincere when you are praying? What does it mean to you to pray in "full assurance of faith"? What part does confession play in your prayers for and with your children? How does your "conscience" affect your prayers?

My Thoughts

_____

_____

_____

_____

_____

_____

_____

_____

_____

_____

_____

_____

Thoughts on Living the Word

The most effective way to teach my children about prayer, I have found, is to pray. It's fairly easy to pray for help on problems, when specific needs arise, for people we know or meet, when a discipline requires confession, or at bedtime. However, I have to train myself to stop and spontaneously give thanks to God for meeting a need, or praise him for a beautiful sunset, or just worship him for who he is. ❧ Whenever I have read a book aloud about someone like George Mueller, or Corrie Ten Boom, or other "heroes of the faith" known for their prayer life, it can influence my children's attitudes toward prayer in new ways. We might even pray differently because of something we pick up on in the book. ❧ It's natural to want to keep a "prayer journal" of asked and answered prayers with children. It's a tangible reminder for them that God is at work in their lives. However, the real purpose of the list should be to generate thanksgiving and praise to a personal, powerful God.

My Life

Personal application: Meditate on Hebrews 4:14-16 for a quiet time this week. Make two columns on a sheet of paper labeled "mercy" and "grace." Identify areas of your homeschooling lifestyle where you need one or the other and write it down. Pray for the things on the list.

Family application: Locate a short biography about the life of George Mueller to read aloud to your children (try the Trailblazers series). When you finish, have an audio-drama tape series to listen to, or a video to watch, about his life. Talk about his prayer life.

"The Christian walk will always be full of problems and work. Many times we must be prepared to suffer willingly... [However], given the ubiquity of overload, we need to choose carefully where our involvement should come...It is not the will of the Father for us to be so battered by the torment of our age."

Dr. Richard A. Swenson
Margin

Chapter Eleven

Light in the Darkness

The Lord is my light and my salvation—whom shall I fear? The Lord is the stronghold of my life—of whom shall I be afraid?

Darkness was slowly overtaking my bedroom, chasing out the last few rays of daylight as evening fell. As the sun slipped behind the horizon, I felt like the light left me as well. I felt a oneness with the gathering darkness, as though it was an expression of my own dark thoughts and feelings. For a long time, I just lay there quietly, staring up at the ceiling, which was rapidly disappearing from my sight as the dim light of dusk turned to dark.

I could easily reach over and turn on my bedside lamp, at least to dispel the darkness of the night, but I didn't want to. After an emotionally-draining, tension-filled day at home, I felt that I deserved this moment of darkness and I didn't need to make it go away. But, also, I didn't turn the lamp on for the simple reason that I didn't want to be found. I just wanted to be left alone. As I lay still in my bed, I wanted to disappear into the darkness like the ceiling, invisible to anyone who might come into the room looking for me. I wanted to escape.

But I couldn't escape my life, and I couldn't escape the dark thoughts rushing around in my mind. Why in the world had God allowed me to be a mother?! Surely he knew I couldn't handle this responsibility. Did he just want me to feel like a complete failure? If so, he sure succeeded. I am totally incapable of being a good homemaker! Undone laundry, dirt and disarray all testify to my disability in this area. And does he know that I'm a hypocrite? Here I am telling thousands of moms how to homeschool when I haven't even done it for the last four weeks myself! And if God meant me to be a mother, why do my children drive me crazy? One more whine, squeal, fuss, or any kind of boy's noise, and I may just scream! Even their childish banter can drive me to the point of distraction. And since children come from having a husband, maybe I never should have gotten married. I wonder sometimes what good I am to Clay. I am just so tired and weary of being so responsible for so much for so long.

I don't normally consider myself a prisoner in my own home, yet I felt like the walls were closing in around me like a prison cell. I had kept a lid on my feelings of desperation for the past few months, but the building tension finally got to me—fussing children, moving boxes everywhere, messes at every turn, a cranky and crying baby, a too-busy husband (who was out of town on this night), grindingly slow homeschooling, and a list of to-dos and demands that strangled my spirit. "That's it! I have nothing more to give. I give up!" I fell into my bed at the end of the day, but what I really wanted was to escape to some unknown place never to be found again.

Eventually, I did turn on the lamp and, out of sheer duty and force of habit conditioned by several thousand bedtime routines, shook off the darkness and kept going. However, I warned my children that I was in no mood to be challenged in any way, nor did I want any child getting out of any bed for any reason at any time this night. Finally, it was quiet and still for the first time that day. I collapsed into my own bed and welcomed the darkness once more before falling quickly, and thankfully, to sleep.

Daylight found its way back into my room the next morning, but it couldn't dispel the darkness in my spirit. I was surprised how exhausted I felt, like I was dragging around a bag of sand as I made my way to the kitchen for my first cup of tea. I stretched out on the living room couch and tried to have a quiet time, but my spirit wasn't in it. One-by-one, the children awoke and gathered around me on the other couches. Their timid expressions and the uncharacteristic hush that had fallen over the room made it clear I needed to relieve their anxiety. They certainly couldn't do anything to relieve mine!

"Kids," I said, trying to keep my emotions in check, "your mother is feeling pretty overwhelmed right now, and I really could use your help." I then began to assign specific household and childcare responsibilities to each child. It was just a bandaid on an emotional cancer, but it was all I knew to do at the moment. The children all took to their respective tasks with a very businesslike demeanor. Their seriousness was surely more reflective of my dark mood than of their real attitude toward work, but it was enough for me that things were getting done. I did my best to work, too, but it was half-heartedly and at a slow pace.

My emotions were pretty dulled for the next couple of days, but not so much that I couldn't see that my children needed some relief from my less-than-chipper mood. So, one cool evening, I suggested we build a good fire in the fireplace, pour some mugs of hot chocolate, and I would read aloud a good novel we had been working through. That was met with smiles, exclamations of approval, and a sudden bustle of activity to make it happen. Nathan's loud voice cut through the din of childish excitement, and with all of his extraverted, exaggerated, exuberant boyish energy he proclaimed, "I think we are the best family in the world, and I feel sorry for other people who don't live like we do!"

I looked at Nathan and simply couldn't help smiling at this darling little boy who was so full of life. Then I looked at my sweet Sarah, and my fun-loving Joel, and my precious Joy. A surge of overwhelming gratitude for each of these precious blessings flowed through my heart. It was as though God was turning the light back on in my spirit. I felt unexplainably and unspeakably blessed as I pondered the priceless treasures before me and the wonderful, warm home God has provided for us. Two days before, I wondered how I could live with them; now I realized I couldn't live without them.

As I lay in bed that night and thought back on the day, I could not find one rational reason to explain my sudden escape from darkness back into the light. What is wrong with me!? Am I schizophrenic? Do I have some kind of hormonal disorder? Am I just immature or unspiritual? How can I feel so emotionally down one day, and then so warmly contented the next, when very little has changed in my life? Why do I get so depressed when I am so blessed? I felt guilty for having had such negative thoughts about everyone, and for having made life miserable for my family for two days. But then guilt in the light is better than depression in the darkness!

I should have known, though, that the bad feelings would pass. Negative thoughts and feelings are just a fact of life, and they come to every person at some time or another. After all, the psalmists poured out much darker thoughts than I did as part of their praise to God. I reminded myself, once again, that having negative thoughts and feelings is not wrong, and they are not necessarily sinful. What I do with those thoughts and feelings, though, will determine whether they become the seeds of increasingly sinful attitudes and actions, or of a stronger spiritual life and dependence upon God. That's why I need to look for God's light when the darkness comes.

৯

It is no real secret privately among homeschooling moms that the struggle with dark thoughts and feelings of depression and despondency is a common experience. What I see publicly, though, is these mothers feeling the pressure to appear to others to have it all together and to be getting everything done. They live under a burden of unrealistic expectations, thinking they need to be exemplary homeschooling mothers, yet daily confronting the reality that they are not. That is hard on the emotions.

Recently, I had tea with a friend, a homeschooling veteran of 14 years. She said that often, when we start homeschooling, we have visions of a family heritage filled with doctors, senators, missionary pioneers, writers, teachers, scientists—each outstanding in every way because of their superior training and education at home. We inadvertently tell the Lord what we expect to get out of our noble decision to homeschool, and subtly expect him to reward our sacrifice. Over time God shows us he has a different plan, and the homeschooling fervor is gradually replaced by the reality that homeschooling can be a tiring, burdensome task. In the end, our children are for the most part pretty average, and we start to wonder if what we have done has mattered at all. Though we have done God's will God's way, we can feel let down and depressed.

As I thought about my friend's insights, I realized that it doesn't stop with just the training and education of our children. Perhaps we are disappointed in our marriages, finding our husband less romantic than we had hoped, not the tower of spiritual strength that we idealized in our minds, or not as involved with the children as we really need. Perhaps our children's personalities are not what we envisioned, or we are disappointed by character weaknesses, lack of social graces, academic underachievement, slowness to learn, or disinterest in certain skills, abilities, or subjects. Perhaps family resources seem irreconcilably inadequate—income, home, car, clothes, books, supportive relatives, church, and friends. Perhaps we feel the sting of rejection or criticism because of homeschooling, especially from Christian friends from whom you expected love and understanding.

All of these issues, and others, can stir up feelings of discouragement, or even of failure. Like Christian in *A Pilgrim's Progress*, you can quickly find yourself getting more and more bogged down in the "slough of despond." You begin to wonder if you will ever really accomplish anything you had hoped for from homeschooling. And the more discouraged or despondent you become, the more difficult it is to climb out of the emotional mire that you've fallen into. It just keeps pulling you down.

But, just as Help came along to aid Christian's escape from the slough of despond, I have found God's help to escape the times of darkness and discouragement that I have sometimes fallen into as a homeschooling wife and mother. A few basic biblical truths have allowed me to draw upon God's grace to escape my despair. I have come to learn that there is light in the darkness, no matter how dark it may seem, when I remember three basic principles of faith. First, I must choose to faithfully depend upon God. Then, I must faithfully obey God. Finally, I must faithfully wait on God.

Faithfully depend upon God

Most negative feelings have some truth to them—children *can* seem burdensome, housework *is* demanding, noise and fussing *is* irritating, moving *is* exhausting, life *can* be overwhelming. The first step to finding light in the darkness is acknowledging that life is hard and sometimes sad, and that we need God to make it through. The Christian life is not a Polly-anna-ish experience, but a process of learning to live by faith in the One who has promised to walk with us through the ups and downs of life, always giving us enough light for the path ahead.

The Apostle Paul certainly had reason to be discouraged many times in his life and ministry. In defending his apostleship to the Corinthian church (2 Cor. 11:22-33), he paints a picture of a life filled with continual rejection, stress, hard work, disappointment, suffering, and deprivation. Yet, the more we read and study the letters of this man of faith, the more we see his utter dependence upon God in the face of seemingly endless difficulties. He was able to live with hope and joy by keeping his focus on the "things above, where Christ is." There was a well-spring of joy, love, and peace in Paul's heart that could come only from a God who was very real to him.

Paul did not dwell on past, or even present, sufferings, both of which were ample in his life. "But one thing I do: Forgetting what is behind and straining toward what is ahead, I press on toward the goal to win the prize for which God has called me heavenward in Christ Jesus." (Phil. 3:13,14). He knew his goal in this life was not to listen to the voices that would lead him to self-pity and depression, but to listen to the voice of God that called him to a life of eternal purpose and reward. That call of God, which was as real to him as the scars he carried from floggings and beatings, enabled him to say with confidence, "I can do everything through him who gives me strength" (Phil. 4:13). He knew that his own strength was not sufficient, but God's strength for him was all sufficient.

The writings of the Apostle Paul have changed the course of countless lives, and even the course of history, by influencing people such as Martin Luther, Hudson Taylor, St. Francis of Assisi, Amy Carmichael, and countless others. Yet when he was alive, Paul could have had no idea of the magnitude and reach of his ministry. None of us is likely to change the course of history, but perhaps the sacrifices and sufferings we accept in Christ's name as homeschooling mothers will change the course of our children's lives. Perhaps our faith in God and dependence upon him will give the world a young man or woman who brings thousands of people into the kingdom of God. We may not see that fruit during our lifetime, but if we keep our focus on the light of our God rather than on the darkness of our feelings, we can "press on toward the goal" and see it in heaven.

There is light for your darkness if you, first, turn to the God of light. He has not turned away from you when darkness covers your spirit—you have turned away from him. There is nothing in this world you can turn to that will "strengthen" you if it turns you away from your God—not your husband, not a better life, not more money or resources, not more mature children, not anything. Only God can strengthen you to do the "all things" that he has asked you to do as a homeschooling mom. "Without faith, it is impossible to please God. For He who comes to God must believe that He is and that He is a rewarder of those who seek Him." (Hebrews 11:6, NASB) Turn to him in faithful dependence—he will reward your faith.

Faithfully obey God

Saying that we believe God is one thing; acting in faith because we believe is quite another. The Old Testament faithful profiled in Hebrews 11, God's Hall of Faith, made the list because of their acts of faith. Abraham, Moses, Rahab, David, the prophets, and the multitudes of faithful believers all testify to the same truth—that true faith is not just professed but expressed. Genuine faith is expressed in a believer's life through obedience to God.

Several years ago, after having been in full-time ministry for 19 years, Clay and I found ourselves facing a faith decision. God had put it on our hearts to start a family ministry, but it was becoming obvious that to do so would mean leaving behind the safety and security of church ministry. That would take a large step of faith. But God gave us a nudge, and by faith we moved to family property near the sleepy Texas town of Walnut Springs, 35 miles from anything that resembled civilization, and 60 miles from a real city. We had no friends, no support systems, no church, no visible means of support, and no clue as to what exactly was going to happen in our future.

Over the next year, my faith was stretched to the limits as I struggled with the reality of what we had done. What if we'd made the wrong decision? Should we really have left good friends, a good church, and a wonderful support group? What if we run out of money? Where will Clay get a job if God doesn't bless our ministry? What if one of us gets really sick? Will my children ever have friends here? Will I? The first year, all three children had chicken pox, meningitis, and a light case of pneumonia, and I suffered my second miscarriage in two years. And for much of that time we were living out of boxes and in the midst of construction.

During that first year, I would take long walks on the country roads near our home to seek the Lord's strength and guidance. I was tempted often to let the dark thoughts push God aside and overwhelm my spirit, but I knew I had to rest in God and stay dependent upon him. The Lord would speak to me quietly in my heart and say, "You have taught the Bible all these years, telling other women to live one day at a time, and to trust me regardless of what comes. That's what you need to do now. It is not my will for you to worry."

All those years of training in Campus Crusade for Christ came back to me as I practiced putting my faith in the facts of God's word and waiting for the feelings to follow. I began to simply obey the scriptures that said, "don't worry about tomorrow," and "be anxious for nothing," and "keep your eyes on Jesus." I knew that if I gave into my fears, I would take life into my own hands by trying to change my circumstances. What I needed was simply to obey God's word and let his Spirit change me through the circumstances. I needed to simply live by faith. By God's grace, that's what I did.

Our feelings never would have led us to Walnut Springs, but our faith did. And that step of obedient faith, and 365 more steps that first year, enabled us to enjoy what God had put on our hearts to do. Despite occasional bouts with unbelief when things looked pretty bleak, God provided for our needs. And despite our many weaknesses and limitations, God providentially built and broadened our ministry. I believe God was responding to our faithful obedience, imperfect though it may have been.

Obedience is rarely easy. More often than not, I don't feel like obeying, and can think of a dozen reasons why not to. But obedience is an act of love for God (John 14:15). I do it because I love God, and he has asked me to. Sometimes it comes down to confessing to God that my heart may not be in it, or my motives may not be completely right, but I am going to obey in faith despite how I feel. As I let his word instruct my mind, and as I determine to obey his word by faith because I love him, I can feel my emotions change. I don't always have immediate victory, but there is light in the darkness. Soon, he responds to my needs, he renews my heart, and he refreshes my spirit. He gives me all the light I need to keep going.

Faithfully wait on God's timing

"The Lord's lovingkindnesses indeed never cease, for His compassions never fail. They are new every morning; great is Your faithfulness. 'The Lord is my portion,' says my soul, 'Therefore I have hope in him.' The Lord is good to those who wait for Him, to the person who seeks Him. It is good that he waits silently for the salvation of the Lord" (Lam. 3:22-26, NASB).

The prophet Jeremiah wrote those words for the people of Israel during one of the darkest and most painful periods of their nation's history. Jerusalem was sacked, the Temple destroyed, a way of life ended, and most of the people either killed, left to die, or taken off to captivity in Babylon. Yet Jeremiah writes to his defeated, desolated people that God's mercies are "new every morning" and that his "faithfulness" is great. Though they have every reason to be hopeless, he tells them to hope in God, and to wait for him, and to seek him. In the blackest days of Israel, God would still be their light in the darkness. But they would have to wait, in faith, to see his salvation.

One of my children, like his mother, has a hard time waiting for anything. If he wants help on a project, he wants it now! He wants instant gratification, and he is passionate about getting his own way. Whatever he feels strongly about, he feels strongly that he is right, and that you should see it his way. It's really just a little older version of how babies operate. If a baby wants something now, he will cry and throw a tantrum. Older children do the same by being impatient and stubborn. Though they think their strong feelings make it right, what it really shows is simply their immaturity and inability to discern their real needs. We learn when we are young to dislike the word "wait."

Early in our marriage, I threw a tantrum or two myself! I didn't want to wait for whatever it was I felt so strongly about. I'm embarrassed, now, to remember some of my self-righteous, immature behavior, yet encouraged that I have matured since then. Still, I am not immune to the dark feelings that spawned my earlier behavior. When I am fatigued, or feeling depressed, I can still become very passionate about my needs or my perspective on life. I can begin to demand my "rights" even though they may be wrong.

When I take those feelings to the Lord in prayer, though, he rarely gives in to my pleadings by immediately answering my prayer. Instead, he usually makes me wait on his answer. And it is during the wait that I begin to hear his voice. He gives me what I really need, rather than what I thought I needed in my immaturity. Waiting gives God's Spirit time to change my attitudes and emotions, and to change my perspective. I usually find I just need to depend on God a little more, and obey him a little better. Coming to that conclusion, though, takes time.

Waiting in the Bible is often synonymous with hope. To wait on the Lord, is to hope in the Lord. Waiting on God does not mean mindlessly and passively passing the time until God does something. Quite the opposite, it means looking ahead with eager anticipation, knowing that God will do something good. Waiting on the Lord is an active, involved process during which the one who is waiting prays, obeys, and trusts God. We would have no reason to seek God if we always got what we wanted when we wanted it. God graciously makes us wait, though, so we will seek him and find him. We sometimes need that extra time to realize he is what we really need.

As David fled from Saul, he had reason to be afraid, to despair, and even to want God to deal swiftly with his oppressor. But in Psalm 27, he expresses a fearless trust in God that seeks him above all else. Though he faces a darkness in his life, he is able to say, "The Lord is my light and my salvation—whom shall I fear?" He prays to and praises his God, and at the close of his psalm expresses his willingness to wait on him. "Wait for the Lord; be strong and take heart and wait for the Lord." Like David, when there is darkness in my life, light comes from waiting on the Lord.

❦

There are seasons of emotions in every woman's life. I know I have had many times of great joy and peace, yet many days of darkness, too. But the more I learn to faithfully depend upon God, obey him, and wait on him, the more light there is when the dark feelings come. As long as I can see his light in the darkness, I know I'll be able to follow as he leads me through it, by faith, one day at a time. He may not change the circumstances that I believe are causing my feelings of darkness, but he will strengthen me to live by faith in the midst of those inevitable challenging circumstances and difficult times. And he will also strengthen me to live by faith in the midst of the mundane tasks that loom large before me every day as a woman, wife, and homeschooling mother.

Like Paul, and David, and so many other faithful Christians, I want to be found faithful in the place where God has placed me. I want to be a faithful source of his light to my children, my husband, and to all who pass by my home. When I face the inevitable times of dark feelings, I want my life to be an example of the truth that God's light shines brightest when it shines in the darkness.

❦

Thoughts On the Living Word

God is pictured numerous times in Scripture expressing emotions. A part of his divine nature is what we call emotion, but it is perfect and without any flaw. Since we are made "in his image," we share that part of God's nature. Emotion—the part of us that experiences happiness, sadness, anger, and shame—is a natural part of life put there by God. However, like so many other "good" things in our lives that God has created, our sin nature messes up our emotions. We are too often tempted to follow our sin-distorted feelings, rather than God. To help us, though, God has put the Holy Spirit in our lives to enable us to live by faith rather than by our feelings. Letting God control even our feelings and passions is a sure mark of Christian maturity. Spirit-controlled emotions and passions drive us to love God and serve others, and that's what makes them good.

Lamentations 3:17-27

Jeremiah laments the destruction of Israel yet he does not lose hope. What was Jeremiah feeling? Have you ever felt like that? How does he overcome his feelings and find encouragement? Would that help you in a difficult time? How? To whom is the Lord "good" and why?

Psalm 73

The psalmist meditates on the fates of the wicked and the righteous. What are some of the words he uses to describe his feelings about the prosperity of the wicked? How do his thoughts and feelings change in the second half of the psalm? Have you ever thought his thoughts? What does he conclude?

1 Corinthians 10:13

Paul cautions his Corinthian readers not to be like the Israelites when God prevented them from entering the land. When are we most vulnerable to a fall? How do passions and feelings heighten our vulnerability? What kinds of emotional "temptations" do we face? Is there any sinful emotion that is inescapable? What is the "way out"?

Philippians 4:4-7

Paul confronts a problem of disunity. What kinds of feelings come from choosing to "rejoice"? What kinds of feelings are countered by "gentleness"? What kinds of feelings replace "anxiety" when you follow this admonition? What kinds of feelings come from "peace"? How does peace "guard your heart"?

My Thoughts

_____

_____

_____

_____

_____

_____

_____

_____

_____

_____

_____

_____

_____

_____

Thoughts On Living the Word

There are a few memory verses in my life that God seems to bring to mind more frequently than others. Whenever I am feeling stressed or anxious, the Holy Spirit pulls Philippians 4:6,7 out of my memory. It almost always changes my attitude or my feelings. It is one of my top-ten recommended memory verses. ❧ I find it a healthy exercise, when my feelings are cratering, to follow the example of the psalmists. I will write out my anxieties, fears, and worries in the form of a prayer to God, or even in the form of a psalm. Though I start with the negatives, my narrative will inevitably move me toward a more mature response to God. ❧ When I'm struggling with my feelings or with negative emotions, the hole just gets deeper and darker if I'm alone in my struggle. It always helps me to find a friend who will be a sympathetic listener and encourager. I need someone else's perspective and companionship when I am down. Sometimes, just getting away for tea and talk with a friend is all I need to get on top of my feelings.

My Life

Personal application: Try writing your own psalm this week in your devotional time. You don't have to be down to do it. Just be honest and expressive with your feelings before God, like the psalmists, and move it toward a response of praise or thanksgiving to him.

Family application: For a family night this week, play charades "with feelings." Each clue must include an emotion—"happy hippopotamus," "sad Solomon," "cheery chickadee." Pictionary with feelings is even more fun as pictures take on faces and expressions.

"When strong winds buffet a tree, it develops strong fiber and relies on its deep root system to withstand storms. This is how we develop fortitude, persistence, and the strength of heart that enable us to meet adversity, pain, and persecution...There is no greater challenge, no higher calling than to persist in the things of God."

William & Nancie Carmichael
Lord Bless My Child

Chapter Twelve

Enduring with Grace

*The Lord is good to those whose hope is in
him, to the one who seeks him; it is good to
wait quietly for the salvation of the Lord.*

C our-a-geous…men…fight…best"—*Lord, how long must I endure
this?*—"when…they…have…no…ill-u-sions." Though I felt like I was about
to burst inside, I kept my composure as Nathan continued to read, word by
word by tedious word. "I…won't…force…any…man… to…stay." I tried
to straighten my leg to relieve an annoying cramp. I had been balled up on
the futon intertwined with my wiggly eight year-old for over half an hour.
My endurance was waning.

"De-clare…your…in-ten-tion…step-ping…over…this…line." Off in
the distance, from the far back bedroom, I could hear baby Joy calling out,
"Mom-my! Momm-my! Mommm-my!" I wanted to go to her, but I let
Sarah answer the call because I didn't want to break Nathan's intense
concentration on his reading. After thirty minutes, he had covered only two-
and-a-half pages, but that was a new milestone in reading for him.

"No…sur-ren-der!…shouted…Colonel…Travis." *Lord, I can't do this
much longer!* It was my own fault, though. I could have just said, "Why
don't you find something easier to read." What possessed me to let him

select a high school reading level book from the library when he was still finding second grade readers challenging? "Lib-er-ty...or...death!" You would think there would be a grade school book about his hero of the Alamo, Colonel William Barrett Travis. But since there wasn't, and I didn't want to disappoint him, I decided to take a chance.

"Travis...fell...grave-ly...wound-ed...on...the...ram-part." Like his Alamo heroes, we fought hard over many words, and each sentence was a major victory. I had to admit that I was amazed at his persistence. As for me, though, I was ready to raise the white flag. I was ready to give up.

But just at that moment, something happened that made all my motherly endurance worth the effort. Nathan looked up at me with an excited smile on his freckly face and said, "Isn't this the neatest book? I think it might be the best book I've ever read! I love reading, Mom! I think I'm just going to read history the rest of my life! Let's keep reading this until we're finished." I was momentarily stunned. I couldn't feel my cramp, I couldn't hear the baby, and I forgot all my griping. Those words, "I love reading, Mom!" just kept ringing in my ears. For the first time in many months, my heart was flooded with a renewed hope.

For about three years, I had been longing to hear those words from my most difficult reading student. This was the child who had so often complained about reading lessons and even reading aloud, interjecting an impatient "Can we be done now?" after only a few minutes of easy reading. This was the child with whom I had lost my patience again and again while trying to do school work with the older ones. This was the child who had left me so frustrated at times that I was tempted to quit speaking about homeschooling because I felt like such a failure. I had endured with my precious extraverted child, hoping that he would one day discover the joy of reading as his older brother and sister had, yet I had grown weary in the task. Now, in one moment, I could see the reward of my endurance. Though there would still be other mountains to climb together, I had a renewed energy and desire to endure with my challenging child.

As I was reading in my Bible later that week, my experience with Nathan put some familiar words into a whole new light for me. "Therefore, do not throw away your confidence, which has a great reward. For you have need of endurance, so that when you have done the will of God, you may receive what was promised." (Heb. 10:35-36, NASB) God spoke these words to Jewish believers who had been driven out of Jerusalem, were discouraged in their faith, and thinking a return to Judaism would deliver them from their suffering.

These embattled Christians were tempted to give up on doing the "will of God." Like them, I have been tempted so many times during our ten years of homeschooling to give up. But if I am doing the will of God by choosing to homeschool my children, then I, too, need to endure. If I throw away my confidence in God—the confidence that he will work in my life and in the lives of my children—then I am throwing away the rewards God wants to give me for doing his will. When I feel like giving up, I may think what I need is divine deliverance, but what I really need is endurance.

We tend to think of endurance as "gutting it out to the end," and there is certainly something of that in the biblical concept. But the Greek word commonly used for endurance is very descriptive. It is a compound word from two Greek words, "under" and "to remain." To endure is to "remain under," or to "bear up under." It is the picture of someone bearing up under the weight of a heavy load on his back. For the Christian, endurance is bearing up under the weight of persecution, or difficulties, or suffering. Although that may sound like gutting it out, true biblical endurance is never just a passive or meaningless exercise. It is always forward-looking. It always has in view a desirable end, a worthy goal, or a divine reward. Biblical endurance is active and purposeful.

As I was pondering the verse in Hebrews, the Lord flooded my mind with memories of many other times when I was tempted to quit homeschooling, but when I needed to endure. I thought of a period of several years in our lives, when we were alone without family nearby or support systems, when ear infections and asthma attacks created a string of sleepless nights, doctors visits, hospital trips, and pharmacy runs. I thought of our many moves, living in and out of boxes, decorating homes for the next resident to enjoy, and wondering how it would affect my children's character and homeschooling. I thought of the months I had to stay in bed because of miscarriages and severe anemia, the two months of bed rest during my last pregnancy, and the recent back injuries from being rear-ended in my car twice within five days.

Those were the "big" interruptions of life, but there also have been the small, daily ones. I needed to endure when my young children disrupted my time with the older ones, when I wondered if anyone was listening to me, and when common denominators and multiplying fractions brought tears of frustration. I needed to endure when character training didn't seem to work, and when rebellious attitudes and sinful fusses derailed my homeschooling. I needed to endure when phone calls knocked the wind out of "good" homeschooling moments, and when broken appliances and other minor catastrophes undermined an entire homeschooling day.

My mind was on a roll now as I thought about enduring the less tangible but more emotionally disruptive interruptions in my life as a homeschooling mother. I needed to endure critics who played on my insecurities by challenging the quality of my children's education, or by warning that my children would need to be prepared for college (gee, never thought of that). I needed to endure strangers, and friends, telling me my children were overprotected and too dependent on me, or that I should think about myself and put them in Christian school, or even that I should not have more than two children because it would keep me from ministry.

As I pondered all these memories, I realized that I could have easily closed the homeschool doors any of a number of times, but I didn't. I chose, instead, to endure the difficulties, not because I had to, but because I truly believed that I was doing God's will, and that God would reward my endurance. I endured by faith.

I knew deep in my heart that God designed me, as a mother, to be at home with my children. To even think of settling for something else would be a step out of his will. No matter how difficult the homeschooling lifestyle might become, my commitment was to do God's will, not my own. Even though I could selfishly choose an "easier" lifestyle, I would have to disobey God to do so. I know in my heart that God has called me to homeschool and that there is no turning back, no matter what today, or the future, holds.

My heart is committed to endure to the end, but I'm thankful that God allows me to see the fruit of that endurance along the way. The greatest reward for my endurance is seeing the hearts of my children growing in godliness and Christian character. It is so fulfilling to see them becoming the kind of people that I would enjoy as friends, knowing that what they are becoming is because I stayed at home with them rather than surrendering them to strangers to shape their hearts and minds. That is the fruit that tastes the sweetest even though it has taken a lot of sacrifice and endurance to produce it.

During a very hectic recent summer, at a time when Clay had to be out of town, the responsibility of a long car trip with all four children fell on me. It was enough to have to pack everything, take it out, and load the trailer. But, the trailer also had to be put onto the hitch, a task I had not yet attempted and was not thrilled about learning at that moment. As I was inside the house making arrangements and worrying about it, ten year-old Joel was taking initiative to do something about it. Without my asking him, he hitched up the trailer by himself (he had watched his dad do it), and loaded all the heavy book boxes. This was a new level of responsibility that I had long been waiting to see in Joel. It was very sweet fruit.

Sarah, my oldest child, has begun to blossom in maturity as she has crossed the threshold from childhood into young adulthood. Her gracious hospitality is a ministry to me and everyone else in the house. When Joel, her younger brother, was sick and in bed with a high fever, she took on his motherly care, bringing him a lovely basket filled with a card, iced ginger-ale, favorite foods, a special book, and topped off with a lovely folded napkin and flower. That fruit tasted so sweet and mature.

Do I taste fruit this sweet every day? Most assuredly not! We struggle daily, even hourly, with bad attitudes, sinful habits, and immaturity. But do I quit because what I desire to see in them comes so slowly and at such a great price of time and effort? No, I endure with them. I know the sweetest fruits of my endurance will be enjoyed only occasionally, but it is enough to keep me pressing on toward the goal of raising mature, godly young men and women. One thing I know for sure—if I don't endure, there will be no fruit to enjoy. So I press on for the goal.

≈

The book of Hebrews was written to Christians, just like you and me, whose faith was being tested daily. They felt like giving up, but the writer told them that they needed to endure, to do the will of God, to live by faith. "We are not of those who shrink back and are destroyed," he said, "but of those who believe and are saved." Oh, Lord, don't let me be one who "shrinks back," giving up on your will for my life because of a lack of faith! Whenever I read those words, my heart cries to God to show me how to endure and persevere, and the writer of the book of Hebrews tells me exactly what to do.

The writer points to the lives of multitudes of heroes of the faith, men and women who persevered through trials and sufferings far greater than anything I have had to face, or likely will have to face. They are a great cloud of witnesses, surrounding me and encouraging me to "run with perseverance" the race marked out for me. They cheer me on, but I am not to look to them as I run. Just as they kept their eyes on God by faith, my eyes of faith are to be looking straight ahead to the object of my faith. I am to "fix [my] eyes on Jesus, the author and perfecter of our faith." He alone is God's answer to the cry of my spirit for help to endure. I am to "consider him who endured such opposition from sinful men, so that you will not grow weary and lose heart." I keep my eyes fixed on Jesus because I know that if I do not I will certainly become weary, lose heart, and give up. The purpose of Christ—to sit down at the right hand of God, having accomplished his work of redemption—was the "joy set before him" for which he "endured the cross, scorning its shame." If Jesus could endure the cross for me, then I can endure the difficulties of this life for him.

I have chosen to homeschool because it is my deep, heartfelt conviction that it is God's will for my life and for my family. If my decision to homeschool was because others are doing it, or because I thought it would be fulfilling, or even because I thought it would be the best education for my children, then I would always be able to choose another option if I got too tired, or overwhelmed, or discouraged. But if my decision to homeschool is because I am being obedient to the design for motherhood and family that I see revealed in Scripture, then I have no other options. My only choice is to obey. If I am living my life by faith, in the power of the Holy Spirit, then I will endure whatever difficulties that choice to obey brings because of the joy set before me. I will faithfully endure so one day I can hear my Lord say, "Well done, good and faithful servant!...enter into the joy of your master."

If you, too, are struggling with the choice you have made to homeschool, just know that is a good sign. If doing God's will was easy, we would have no need of faith, and no need of God. God knows that we will not trust him until we have to. What you need is not deliverance from your difficulties, but "you have need of endurance." The writer of Hebrews says right before that, though, that we should "encourage one another—and all the more as you see the day approaching." Mutual encouragement will help us endure until the Lord's return. Let me share a few thoughts and verses that I hope will encourage you as you fix your eyes upon Jesus, do his will, and look for his return.

Walk by faith, not by sight

It is so easy to fall into the habit of walking by sight as a parent. It seems I too often "see" only what is wrong with my children, or with myself, but not what could be right. I have 20/20 vision when it comes to looking at flaws and imperfections, but I act as though I am blind when it comes to looking at future potentials. And if I turn my gaze upon myself, I see only my inadequacies and failures as a parent. It's as though I am walking down a path in a forest and looking only at my feet, telling myself when to put the next foot forward, how far to step, how hard, and anxiously trying to make each step the very best that it can be. I am walking only by sight. If I were walking by faith, I would be looking up at what is around me, and looking ahead to where I am going, simply letting God direct my feet. I may not be able to see the destination, but when I am looking for it I walk more confidently.

The Apostle Paul, in 2 Corinthians 5:7, reminds his readers that it is easy to be fooled into looking at the "things which are seen," but which are passing away, rather than looking at the "things which are not seen," which are eternal. When we look to anything in this world for our confidence, we will slowly and surely "lose heart." When my focus is on whether or not my children are mature enough, how far we've come or have to go in homeschooling, or how effective or ineffective I am as a parent, I soon lose heart and become discouraged. Why? Because I am trying to put my faith in things that are "passing away." But if I look to the "unseen" by faith, even "momentary, light affliction" produces confidence because my focus is on the Lord. My faith is anchored in the eternal. That is why he says, "we walk by faith, not by sight."

God has encouraged me through the years not to look at my children as they are at any point in time, but as what God is making them. I have to look with eyes of faith to see beyond the momentary rough edges that God will need time to smooth out. For nearly three years, I had to look beyond Nathan's resistance to reading and, by faith, see that God was working in the "unseen" areas of his life. If I had "walked by sight" with him, I would have driven his resistance deeper by nagging and pressuring him to read. But I "walked by faith," confident that God was at work. He was.

Live one day at a time

Have you ever caught yourself worrying about the future? You're helping a child with math when you hit a snag with decimals. You become frustrated because your child just can't seem to "get it" so you can move on. You start to think what it's going to be like in a few years when you hit algebra and geometry, and you won't have all the answers. You envision your child doing poorly in math, maybe even being handicapped for college. Now you're really worried, and it only redoubles your frustration in working on the decimal problems.

I can fall into this kind of "future worry" trap so easily, whether it is feeling overwhelmed from trying to imagine myself making it through chemistry or calculus, or just having to teach one more child to read. Worrying about what hasn't yet happened, or even about what very well might happen tomorrow, chokes the life out of whatever is happening today. When you worry about tomorrow, you are, in effect, saying that today is not worth enjoying. That is not a message I want to send to my children. I have found only one way to live, and that is to live one day at a time. It sounds trite, I know, but it's also biblical.

"Who of you by worrying can add a single hour to his life?...Therefore do not worry about tomorrow, for tomorrow will worry about itself. Each day has enough trouble of its own." Worrying, as Jesus teaches in his Sermon on the Mount, adds nothing to your life. It only subtracts from your ability to live well today. He doesn't suggest that living in the present means you won't face difficulties, but just that it is senseless to borrow worry from a future that hasn't happened. His antidote to worry is a life of faith: "But seek first his kingdom and his righteousness, and all these things will be given to you as well" (Matt. 6:33). In other words, make your priority whatever God is doing in your life right now. Seek him today, while you can. If you do, then "all these things," even the homeschooling things you think you have to worry about, will be provided in God's timing and way. Live for today, trust him for tomorrow.

I have found that God will give me grace to face today, and for whatever tomorrow holds his grace will still be in ample supply when it comes. I am not like Scarlet O'Hara, passing off the future with a flippant "fiddle-dee-dee." Rather, I want to be like Corrie Ten Boom, confident that the God who provides me the moment-by-moment grace to live for today, will also take care of whatever tomorrow brings. I want to live life one day at a time, and live each day to the fullest measure of the grace that I am given.

Accept trials as from God

As a brand new Christian, I prayed that God would use me to minister to many people. Though I sincerely loved God and wanted to do his will, there was also a part of me that wanted some of the glory for what Sally Bone could do for him. But God, knowing my real needs, gave me instead many years of difficulties and trials. He knew that my real need was to be humbled, so that I would take my eyes off myself, trust him, and find the fulfillment and joy of knowing him that nothing in this world can provide, not even having a great ministry in his name.

The older I get, the closer I get to my Lord, and the more I see what he is like—his greatness, holiness, righteousness, mercy, love, and grace. The more I know him, the more I understand that the trials and difficulties he allows in my life are for my good, just as he has humbled me through the years to draw me closer to him. I understand James 1:2-4 so much better now as a seasoned, mature Christian: "Consider it all joy, my brethren, when you encounter various trials, knowing that the testing of your faith produces endurance. And let endurance have its perfect result, that you may be perfect and complete, lacking in nothing" (NASB).

God tests my faith in many ways—yes, even in homeschooling—in order to make it stronger. If it is true faith, it will result in endurance. And if I endure, then I will become more mature ("perfect and complete"), and closer to God. And if I am closer to God, then I truly am "lacking in nothing." And that is cause for me to "consider it all joy."

Though I am not yet "perfect and complete," and God obviously is still working on me to prove my faith and build my endurance, I can confidently confess the words of James 1:12: "Blessed is the man who perseveres under trial; for once he has been approved, he will receive the crown of life, which the Lord has promised to those who love Him" (NASB).

As I endure and persevere in the difficulties God allows in my life, especially those of my own making, I see him at work in my life to make me more like Jesus and to prepare me for heaven. I am reminded that God's real goal for my life is not that I receive the approval of men, but that I receive the approval of my gracious Lord when he places on me the crown of life eternal. He will be pleased, not because of all the wonderful things Sally did in his name in this life, but because I endured to the end, doing his will and loving him, finding joy even in the trials because they drew me closer to my Lord.

꙳

We don't too much like the word today, but during the Victorian era "duty" was a valued virtue. To perform one's duty meant that a person did what he was supposed to do, because it was the right thing to do, regardless of his feelings or the personal cost associated with that duty. Colonel William B. Travis of the Alamo was raised with that sense of duty. He was just a young man in his mid-twenties, but when duty called, he gave his life because of it.

It was common in the last century for good parents to train their children with a strong sense of duty in life, and expect them to live up to their duties. In a sense, endurance is the duty of living by faith. It is doing what I should do, regardless of how I feel or what it costs, because it is what God wants me to do. If I want my children to adopt the same sense of duty toward God that I feel, they must see me fulfilling my duty to them, even when it is difficult.

In my homeschool, it is my duty to endure with my children through the algebra and fraction problems ahead, the spelling mistakes, the many days of bad attitudes, the tears of frustration, and many other battles to be fought aong the way. When they come, though, I'll just bring to my mind Nathan's sweet, freckly, eight year-old face smiling up at me saying, "I love reading, Mom!" And with his hero, Colonel Travis, I'll say in my heart, "No surrender!"

I don't know exactly what lies ahead of me in my life, or even how my children will turn out, but I know with certainty what my "duty" is before God. Despite the certainty of difficulties and struggles along the way, I must faithfully endure. If I do I will find, at the end of this path called life, the God who has faithfully walked with me every step of the way. And then I will see the eternal fruit of my faith.

"Therefore, my dear brothers (and sisters!), stand firm. Let nothing move you. Always give yourselves fully to the work of the Lord, because you know that your labor in the Lord is not in vain" (1 Cor. 15:58).

God has promised that he will accomplish far more through you and me than we can even imagine, if we choose to faithfully endure. Let's choose together to live by faith, "so that when you have done the will of God, you may receive what was promised."

❧

Thoughts On the Living Word

Endurance is not just a biblical concept. Anyone who is alive, whether they belong to God or not, knows that our days on this earth are an endurance run. For those of us who belong to God, though, we run not just to make it through life, but to make it to eternal life. We know that God is watching, and that our endurance will be rewarded, so we endure in faith with our eyes on the goal. For those without God, the end of their endurance is just that…an end. Endurance is their only real hope to make it through this life, but in the end there is no payoff. For the Christian, our endurance leads not to an end, but to a beginning. We can endure because we have hope in the life to come.

Hebrews 10:35-39

The writer encourages Jewish Christians who are struggling to keep their faith. What "reward" has God "promised" to those who endure, or persevere? What would make you want to "shrink back" from the life of faith? What reasons do you have to want to "persevere"? How does God want you to endure and persevere as a Christian mother?

Hebrews 12:1-3

The writer points his readers to Jesus, the "author and perfector" of our faith. Do you feel like you are winning your "race"? What keeps you from running the race with endurance, or perseverance? What are some of the sins that can "entangle" you? What things in your life "hinder" you and weigh you down? How can you ensure that you will not "grow weary and lose heart"? Do you do that?

Galatians 6:7-10

Our endurance is not just to get us through life, but to live it for God, people, and the gospel. How does the principle of "sowing and reaping" apply to endurance? What does it mean to persevere in "doing good"? What will we reap if we do not "give up"? What are you sowing in the lives of your children?

Isaiah 40:27-31

Isaiah encourages the Israelites to persevere. How does it encourage you to know that God is always watching, never tiring? How has God given "strength" when you were "weary," or "power" when you were "weak"? What does it mean to you to "hope in the Lord"? How does that affect your children?

My Thoughts

Thoughts On Living the Word

If I want to be a good runner in the Christian life, I have to be in good condition. I have found it helpful to take some time alone to evaluate my life following the pattern of Hebrews 12:1-3—read about a hero of the faith; identify whatever slows me down as a runner; confess any sins that are tripping me up; read the gospels and meditate on Christ's life. ❧ Clay and I also make sure that we are each getting enough rest, and even some "off track" time alone and together. Just like in a real race, good nutrition and good health will increase your spiritual endurance, too. ❧ One thing that really keeps me going, though, is to know I'm not running alone. Clay and I encourage and strengthen each other as we run the race of the Christian life together—discussing the scriptures, praying together, sharing our struggles and victories, and helping each other keep going. In the same way, I need kindred-spirit friendships with other women who will offer me encouragement and understanding when I need strength to endure.

My Life

Personal application: Invite several other homeschooling mothers who you consider trusted friends to your house. Discuss Hebrews 10:32-12:3. Share together what has enabled you to keep going during difficult times. Pray for each other.

Family application: Have a Race of Faith family night. Create a timed course that each family member must run with extra clothing, a heavy backpack, and a rope around their legs. Then run it without one or all of those things. Afterward, talk about Hebrews 12:1-3.

Postscript

The life of a mother is so full of seasonal changes. Every day, her heart must adjust to whatever new winds are blowing through her life, whether they are warm or cold, dry or wet, calm or catastrophic. It wouldn't be so bad if life really happened like the seasons, each following predictably after the other. Then you could at least have a reasonable expectation of what kinds of winds would be blowing through your family this week, and the next. But they do not. They are anything but predictable.

A mother's life is a whirlwind of seasons, changing from one to another without much warning, and then to another the next day. If your heart is prepared, you can adjust to whatever season comes upon you, weathering the changes with faith and grace; if your heart is not prepared, you will find yourself reeling and twisting in the winds of life, grasping for something or someone to hold onto.

But that is the secret to weathering the seasons of life. You need something—God's word, and someone—Jesus Christ, to hold onto. They are what give you the grace to weather the seasons. Nothing else can—not a person, not a lifestyle, not a pill, not a place, not a thing. Only the revealed truth of God made alive in your heart through the Holy Spirit can.

That reality is what lies behind the title of this book, *Seasons of a Mother's Heart*. The thoughts and stories on these pages are some of the seasons that I have experienced as a mother, what I have learned from them, and how they have prepared my heart for the wonderful task of motherhood. My hope is that you will find encouragement and strength through them. If I have succeeded in pointing you to the Lord and to the Scriptures as the real sources of that strength, then I know you will.

In the end, it is my prayer that you will come away from this book with a renewed vision for your role as a Christian mother. I want you to come away thinking that your life has great meaning and significance because of the stewardship of your children that God has entrusted to you. He has placed into your hands young lives who one day might influence an entire generation because of your faithfulness to God's design for motherhood. Within your children's hearts and minds will be messages of faith, hope, and love, impressed there by you, that will touch and change lives far from your own, and even long after you are gone. Your light will never go out as long as it continues to burn in the lives of your children.

That is what makes the changing seasons of your life meaningful and purposeful. God uses them to accomplish his purposes in your life, and through you in the lives of your children. The seasons are not to be resisted, but rather welcomed and embraced. It is through them, not in spite of them, that your faith will be strengthened and perfected, and that the faith of your children will be cultivated and grown. The seasons of your heart are the means by which God will prepare you and your children for his work, both now and for generations to come.

May we all, as mothers after God's heart, seek his face, know his heart, and be yielded to his will for our homes and families.

ا◆

Postscript: Ten Years Later

In every season of my life as a mother over the last ten years, my heart has grown steadily stronger in my commitment to God's design for mother-hood. In the decade since I first published this book for homeschooling mothers, God has opened doors for three more books to encourage all mothers, and given me opportunities to encourage thousands of moms here and around the world through speaking, and even through the internet. Like

Lady Wisdom in Proverbs, I am compelled now to lift up my voice and call out to mothers everywhere to hear God's heart for them, to return to and to build their homes, and to find the heartfelt fulfillment of the simple wisdom of God's design for mothers. God is calling out for faithful mothers, and I am blessed to be part of such a company of the faithful.

When you come home to God's design, though, you will experience all of the calms and storms of all of the seasons. Life as a mother, following God's heart, is not a trip to the beach in a season-less tropical paradise. It's real life, true life, as God intended it to be. He will use all the seasons to shape and challenge your heart, to prepare you to be a mother after his heart, and to equip you to raise wholehearted children for Christ who will follow him, and then do the same for their own children. It is your calling. You are a strategic link in God's plan for building his family—those he calls his children, and who will spend eternity with him.

May God grant you the courage to stay true to your vision for being a godly mother. May you find grace, strength, and love from God to sustain you in all the seasons of your heart as a mother, and to empower you to raise children whose hearts will be resilient, responsive, and committed to the cause of Christ. May he guard your heart from the evil one, and fill you with his Holy Spirit to keep your heart strong and faithful for him, until you see him face to face. And may we all, as mothers, look forward together to seeing the fruit of our seasons when we reach our eternal home in heaven.

> *I pray that the eyes of your heart may be enlightened, so that you will know what is the hope of His calling, what are the riches of the glory of His inheritance in the saints, and what is the surpassing greatness of His power toward us who believe.*

❧

1998

2003

2008

About Sally Clarkson

Sally and Clay Clarkson were married in 1981, and have four children—Sarah, Joel, Nathan, and Joy. They have lived in Texas, southern California, Colorado, and Tennessee, and as missionaries in Vienna, Austria. They founded Whole Heart Ministries in 1994 to encourage and equip Christian parents to raise wholehearted Christian children at home. Sally was teaching about homeschooling before she had her first child in 1984, and wrote the first edition of *Seasons of a Mother's Heart* when her children were all 13 and under. At the time of this new Ten Year Anniversary edition, one child is still at home (Joy, 12), and three have graduated.

Sally completed her degree in English and Speech at Texas Tech University in 1975, and joined the staff of Campus Crusade for Christ the summer after graduation. Her time on staff included two years of campus ministry at the University of Texas, three years in Eastern Europe, and then ministry to executive women and single adults in Denver, Colorado, where Clay was on the singles leadership team while attending Denver Seminary. Sally remained active in ministry after their marriage, and has been involved in discipleship and teaching ministries to women, twenty-eight WholeHearted Mother Conferences, numerous home education workshops, and speaking nationally and internationally. Sally is also the author of *The Mission of Motherhood* and *The Ministry of Motherhood* with WaterBrook Press, and *The Mom Walk* with Harvest House Publishers.

Sally's heart's desire is to biblically encourage, inspire, and motivate Christian mothers, and especially homeschooling mothers. Her messages are filled with personal warmth, biblical insights and inspiration, and practical help. Discipleship is the heartbeat of her life and messages. To stay in touch with mothers through the internet, Sally also posts regularly on her weblogs (blogs), www.ITakeJoy.com and www.MomHeart.com.

Sally enjoys good friends, books of all kinds, beautiful art, Celtic and acoustic music, old movies, evening walks, traveling, strong English tea in a china cup, Austrian coffee, and baking whole wheat breads and rolls.

Whole Heart Ministries

Keeping Faith in the Family

Whole Heart Ministries is a non-profit Christian home and parenting ministry dedicated to helping Christian parents raise wholehearted Christian children. Other books and resources by the Clarksons include:

The Mission of Motherhood, by Sally Clarkson
Following God's biblical design for motherhood. (WaterBrook Press)

The Ministry of Motherhood, by Sally Clarkson
Ministering to your children by the example of Jesus. (WaterBrook Press)

The Mom Walk, by Sally Clarkson
Encouragement for walking with God as a mother. (Harvest House)

Educating the WholeHearted Child (3rd Ed.), by Clay & Sally Clarkson
Home education handbook for "WholeHearted Learning." (WH Press)

Books for the WholeHearted Family, by Sarah Clarkson
Wholehearted whole books list for book-loving families. (WH Press).

Journeys of Faithfulness (revised), by Sarah Clarkson
Stories and studies of four faithful single women in Scripture. (WH Press)

Our 24 Family Ways Family Devotional Guide, by Clay Clarkson
A biblical family values discipleship and devotional tool. (WH Press)

Whole Heart Family Classics Collection, by Clay Clarkson, editor
Unburied treasures back in print from ca. 1860-1920. (WH Press)

Path of Life Parenting, by Clay Clarkson
Revised edition of *Heartfelt Discipline* on biblical parenting. (WH Press)

I Take Joy, blog hosted by Sally Clarkson (www.itakejoy.com)
Inspirational encouragement and biblical insights for Christian women.

Mom Heart, blog hosted by Sally Clarkson (www.momheart.com)
Inspirational encouragement, helps, and insights for Christian mothers.

Whole Heart Ministries
P.O. Box 3445
Monument, CO 80132

888-488-4HOME (4466)
whm@wholeheart.org
www.wholeheart.org